# A WALK
## to BACK WHEN
*short stories of my life. . .*

## ALICIA M. SHARPTON

xulon
PRESS

*A Walk To Back When*
*short stories of my life. . .*
by Alicia M. Sharpton

Printed in the United States of America

ISBN 9781498463638

Cottontown, TN 37048
Original Stories by Alicia M. Sharpton
Editing by Terre Rock Beck

www.xulonpress.com

# DEDICATION

*I*n the fall of 1996, my son introduced me to an amazing young woman by the name of Carla Sue Anna Callaway. Instantly our spirits bonded and we became friends. Throughout the time I knew her she became my little sister, my very best friend and an honorary member of our immediate family!

On August 22, 2011, Carla went to be with the Lord. Her death not only shocked all that knew her, but left a tremendous void only God can ever fill!

I am blessed because of Carla. She lives on because of the memories I am able to revisit. Many of our times together are included in this book. Story after story capture just a piece of what we shared. I am thankful for her love, her support and her friendship. Her life has impacted my life in an incredible way. I am thankful to God for allowing our paths to have crossed and remained parallel for as long as they did. I am in great anticipation of our reunion in Heaven, one sweet day.

This book is dedicated to her memory.

*Carla Sue Anna Callaway*
*December 21, 1978–August 22, 2011*

# ACKNOWLEDGEMENTS

Without my family and close friends, many of the following stories would not have even occurred. The numerous laughs exchanged along with the heart-wrenching tears of sorrow have been the thread that has bound together the memories of my life.

*To the following, I give you my thanks. . . .*

~ To My Heavenly Father . . . for purposing my life, loving me unconditionally and seeing the perfected me. Thank you for choosing me to hold the pen as you dictated the words on the following pages. I am honored to be your servant!

~ My Parents . . . for giving me a childhood filled with great memories, a Christian heritage and attributes from the two of you that have made the greatest part of me!

~My Husband, Gary . . . for allowing me to be me! Thank you for believing in what God instructed me to do and for letting me go for it. I love you!!!

~ My Children and Grandchildren . . . for being the greatest gift God could have ever given me. You are my strength and inspiration.

~ Terre Rock Beck . . . for the precious gift you are to me. Words can never express my gratitude for your willingness to hear the challenge God laid before me, walk beside me along the way and your help in bringing to completion this very book He purposed.

~ My Family and Friends . . . for your faithfulness to always be a breath of fresh air in my life. Thank you for your prayers and belief in me even when you could feel the splinters from my roughness. I am still a work in progress.

# ACKNOWLEDGEMENTS

# INTRODUCTION

*"I have been crucified with Christ and I no longer live, but Christ lives in me.*
*The life I now live in the body, I live by faith in the Son of God,*
*who loved me and gave Himself for me."*
*Galatians 2:20 (NIV)*

Writing poetry since I was a teenager, I was confident this was all God intended for me to do. Years later, however, He called me to an even greater task. He challenged me to take a look back on my life and recall His provision, presence and power in my history. For a time, He allowed me to see through His eyes where His hand had delivered me. In my observation, I have witnessed firsthand the evidence of His fingerprints on my heart. As far back as childhood, I have seen where His footprints walked before me preparing the way for my lifelong journey.

Clinging to His cloak, I have traveled thus far 57 years, on this unpredictable road, in this barren land. The stories compiled in this book are not make-believe. They are actual accounts of events that have taken place in my own life.

As you journey with me, through the following pages of time, may you be inspired, enlightened, and intrigued by the ever-presence of our Heavenly Father. May you, too, take time to see where God has illuminated the path upon which you have trod throughout your life. If you will continue looking for His light, He promises to lead your way!

More In Love With Him,
Alicia Sharpton

# ONE BY ONE

Fortunately, my personality allows me the ability to cross the paths of those who will be life-long friends. I cannot even begin to imagine my journey through life without them. Not only do we share our deepest secrets, we know one another inside and out. God has taken every inch of me and placed a friend that relates to every single part. All unique, He has provided that one who could pull out of me the good, the great, and the crummy. God has indeed met every need I have ever faced! It is through those priceless ones I have experienced times of joy through laughter. There have also been occasions that they have felt the sprinkle of my tears. Both happiness and sorrow have deepened and tied together the bond we'll always have.

As the years go by, there are those who I no longer live around. My address book and cell phone host the names and numbers of many friends that trace back as far as high school. Often God will bring them to mind and I will stop for a moment to recall a place and time from the past. With a mixture of emotion, I will find myself lost in time with a special sister. Picking up the phone or sending a card or text, we can re-stitch our hearts with memories as we recall them together. Catching up on the present and reminiscing on the past, we are again thankful for the blessing of becoming friends.

As you read this book, you will know if you are one of those special friends who have journeyed with me. I take this moment to thank you for our time. I thank you for your willingness to have walked with me thus far. Although we never knew where we were going, God did. We may meet again or possibly not, but I thank you with all of me for our own special memories, places and adventures. Your influence has made me the person God has purposed me to be.

Today, take time to step into the past. Allow God to remind you of those He has planted in your path. May you spend sweet moments recalling your history as you think of the memories preserved from your yesteryears!

*"A friend loves at all times, and a brother*
*is born for a time of adversity."*
*Proverbs 17:17 (NIV)*

# TABLE OF CONTENTS

### My Childhood

## Young Adulthood

## The Rest of the Stories

# MY CHILDHOOD

# What Happened To The Directions?

*I* have countless memories of childhood. Some good. Some not so good. One in particular, haunts me until this day.

Our family lived in a three-bedroom house in LaGrange, Georgia. I was probably four years old and my sister two. As does today, the winter often ushers in a nasty head and chest cold. Fortunately in the present day, we have every kind of over-the-counter medicines to remedy the illness. When I was a little girl that was not the case! My mother had her own idea of miracle cures and the one she used on our head and chest cold was torturous and unbelievable to most! The over-the-counter "Vicks Vapor Rub" was her cure. I might also add, her very best friend. I'm convinced of it! The operative word is *rub*! Unfortunately for my sister and I, she missed the *rub* part. Instead of rubbing us down, we had to swallow a spoon full. By chance, have you ever noticed the consistency of that stuff? It's ridiculously thick! That's why they call it a *rub*! Somehow, though, my mom obviously failed to recognize that important fact.

Thankfully, my sister and I didn't choke to death while digesting it. Gratefully we were able to recover from the trauma of being forced to swallow such nasty tasting stuff. Honestly, I'd much rather have endured the uncomfortable misery of the cold than ever had to swallow anything with that consistency.

Truthfully, my mom was really convinced that this medical approach was a sure fire cure. I, on the other hand, would totally disagree. In life, we all tend to become assured of something that is a miraculous cure. We swear by it, trust in it, and claim it as the answer. Sometimes, even when we think it's something other's may not, we force it on anyone. We become so passionate about it that we fail to see the lasting effect it may have on our very own audience. Forcing the issue down another's throat may turn them away for life. Making our point the only answer could very well block their view forever seeing the true benefits in their life.

My mom and I laugh about it now. I can hardly stand to look at a jar. Because I trust my mom, I know her judgment was one of making me better. In life though, do we always strive to see that our judgments aren't forceful ones? Are we acting out of sincere concern or just trying to prove our point? Stand back today. Take a look around and inventory your actions. Be assured of your genuine concern for others. Make certain your solutions really are cures for common life miseries and not simply a way of forcing your beliefs down another's throat.

*"So that there should be no division in the body, but that*
*its parts should have equal concern for each other."*
*1 Corinthians 12:25 (NIV)*

# Holding Me Down

When I was four years old and my sister two, we lived in a little one bedroom home in LaGrange, Georgia. Our kitchen was small but kids can play anywhere. Chasing each other around the kitchen table, somehow my feet came out from under me. With no way of bracing myself, my chin hit the corner of our wooden table slicing it open. Slamming onto the floor, I could see the blood dripping onto my clothes.

Screaming, my mom and dad came running to see what all the commotion was about. In total shock from the sight of the blood, my sister just stood there. Picking me up and cleaning up my chin, it was evident I had to have stitches. In those days, a hospital visit was required and sewing it up was the remedy. Luckily, unaware of what was about to happen, I obediently got into the car and we drove to the Emergency Room.

Arriving, the nursing staff, along with my dad, walked me back to a room. I was much calmer by then but still unsure of what was about to happen. Placing me up on the table, and laying me back to access my cut, the horror began. Before I knew it, arms from everywhere were coming at me. Holding my legs, holding my face, holding my arms and holding my chest, I could not have moved if I had tried. Hearing my daddy try to comfort me didn't help either. I couldn't even see him for all the faces around me looking down at me. I was in pain and scared! Holding me down and keeping me still was essential to stitch my cut. No numbing just sewing. I was so tired by the time the procedure was complete. I had used every ounce of energy.

Being held captive on that table was so scary as a little girl. It was not until the procedure was over and my father picked me up that I felt secure. I ultimately knew the worst had past and I was finally going home! Today, I still have a scar from my fall. Every time I see it, it is a sobering reminder of that horrible experience so many years ago!

Have you memories of a situation where you had to endure loss of control? Do you recall a traumatic time in your past when you were so afraid? Take time today to realize, unlike our earthly fathers, we have a Heavenly Father who can comfort us in our devastating times. He always walks beside us ready to hold our hands. And in the most frightening moments, He guarantees to comfort, protect and go with us through anything we experience. For it's by His strength that we are made strong. Thank Him today for always being there.

*"He said, 'Don't be afraid, friend. Peace. Everything is going*
*to be all right. Take courage. Be strong.' Even as He*
*spoke, courage surged up within me. I said, 'Go ahead,*
*let my master speak. You've given me courage.'"*
*Daniel 10:19 (The Message)*

# His Security

*A*s a young child, I was somewhat of a shy, quiet girl. My self-esteem level probably reached below the halfway mark on the scale. I specifically remember surrounding myself with those people who made me feel confident.

My mother always said that my shyness was apparent even as young as four years old. My parents enrolled me in dance classes, hoping to help me meet some new little friends that could help me step out of my shyness. I went to class but not alone. I refused to go by myself, so my mother and younger sister also went with me. She might have cared about me stepping out from my shyness, but I could have cared less! All I was afraid of was her leaving me alone in a room filled with strangers!

Because my mother was one to complete what she had started, the three of us went to dance class every week. At the end of the lessons, there was still one major hurdle. The dance recital! Although I had accomplished learning the routine, getting on the stage was another story. Cleverly, as my class and I stepped onto that stage, my mother stood behind the curtain, holding my sister and holding my hand! Yes, with my mother's hand grasping mine, I was able to successfully finish the routine and complete the class!

Still, at times feeling that little girl inside, my feelers are always out. I am always drawn to those around me who, too, may be in the midst of uncertainty in their environment. God has used my own insecurities to help secure those who need that hand. Those that can use that very hand, like my mother's, that was extended to me. My Heavenly Father has equipped my heart to be a life vest of sorts to pull in another brother or sister who could possibly become a victim of drowning. It is through my willingness to reach out that God can use me. It is that obedience that allows me to serve on the rescue squad while bringing someone to the Master.

What about you? Have you been in a rescue mode lately? Is God leading you to help relate, restore, or revive the heartbeat of someone through that of the Living God? Ask Him today. Allow the Lord to use your insecurities to be a security to someone in need today.

*"Just as the Son of Man did not come to be served, but to*
*serve, and to give His life as a ransom for many."*
*Matthew 20:28 (NIV)*

# HER COMING HOME

There is something deep in our gut that brings sadness and loneliness when we are without our loved ones. That first experience for me goes all the way back to my childhood. Although my sister and I fought, were jealous and experienced all the normal emotions and feelings all sisters do, I still loved her. She was a piece of me. She was my playmate. She was family.

When my sister was two, she had several bouts with sore throats. Eventually, she had to be hospitalized to have her tonsils removed. My mom's mom came to our house from Roswell, Georgia to take care of me. It was a long few days! Life just wasn't the same. I ate alone, played alone, watched cartoons alone, sat alone, and cried alone. I missed my sister. Being so young, I could not even go to the hospital to visit my companion! It seemed like forever that my entire family had been away. Although my grandmother was with me, it just wasn't the same.

Finally after a few long lonely days, my grandmother and I sat anxiously on my front porch swing as we watched down the hill at the traffic light. I didn't flinch as I waited for the sight of my daddy's car. This time it was different. It wasn't my daddy coming home from work but him bringing my sister home! Her surgery was over. Knowing I still had to allow her to heal, at least she was finally going to be home with me again!

Sure enough, the red light turned green and my daddy's car drove up the hill into our driveway. Running out to the car, I couldn't get the door opened fast enough. My sister was pale looking and needed more recovery but she was there. I was so relieved things were going to be getting back to normal. That they did. We fought, played, shared and experienced everything we had before. This time was different though. We did it in more appreciative love than before. We had grown from our separation. She missed me as much as I missed her. Even though our personalities clashed at times we were still sisters! We also quickly realized that we were very best friends!

God created us for relationships. Although He offers Himself as our very best friend, He knows our desire for fleshly friends. Because of that, He is faithful to provide those too. He sends people in our lives that will enhance us, share with us, teach us and love us with His love.

When was the last time you thanked God for your relationships? When was the last time you thanked God for being your very best friend? And, if He isn't, take time to make Him the center of your life today!

*"And the scripture was fulfilled that says, 'Abraham believed*
*God, and it was credited to him as righteousness,'*
*and he was called God's friend."*
*James 2:23 (NIV)*

# ALL OUR TRAVELS

One of the things I specifically remember about childhood is the many trips enjoyed by our family. It seemed we were always going somewhere. Whether to Florida camping, a family reunion, or just to visit relatives, it seemed we were always on the road. I can also remember one particular sight we were sometimes able to see. It was a sight to us that was a treat!

Nestled in the back of an old truck, on the side of the road, was an old man with a white beard. In the bed of the truck, he stored all of his belongings and his pet goats. Yes, the goats were his companions. They traveled with him. He had traveled around enough that the word had gotten out and he became known as the official, "*Goat Man*." Once seeing him, my daddy would always stop the car. My sister and I were then able to go talk to him and see his animals. With my parents, we looked inside the back of his truck to see the hay and all of his stuff. Knowing his living conditions were certainly not what we were use to, there was just something interesting about this man.

As an adult, I realized that the "*Goat Man*" wasn't really meant to be a sideshow. It was the actual home of a man who had no home. He and his goats along with everything he owned lived in his truck because he was poor. When people stopped to see what I thought was an attraction, they were stopping to give him money. Money to eat. I never even knew. I never saw or realized the true story of his situation.

Isn't life often that way? Sometimes we go through difficulties that others know nothing about. It's not until we have the full knowledge of someone's history that we can really understand his or her story. Things, people and situations may seem one way but in reality, they are nothing like we imagine. Judging from sight is a poor way of assessing anything or anybody. Without all the details, no story can be complete. God reminds us that He looks at the heart. He sees us in His image instead of the way we see ourselves.

Take time today to look around for those you perhaps have falsely judged. Take time to weigh the reality of someone's story being one you've never really heard. Take time to readjust your thinking. Borrow God's eyes for a little while and look at the people around you differently. Allow God to remind you there is much more to the story than you may have never known!

*"But the Lord said to Samuel, "Do not consider his appearance or height, for*
*I have rejected him. The Lord does not look at the things people look at.*
*People look at the outward appearance, but the Lord looks at the heart."*
*1 Samuel 16:7 (NIV)*

# SWEET MEMORIES

When I was a little girl, often I would hide in my MawMaw and Papa's back porch closet. This closet was gigantic to my small eyes. With large wooden planks that served as shelves, my grandmother neatly stacked her folded handmade quilts. Each one was fashioned with it's very own colors, shapes, and size. For me to fit in this massive closet, my climbing skills had to be in tack. When finally reaching the top of all of those quilts, I would be able to literally touch the ceiling. I can still recall the softness as those blankets surrounded my small girlish frame. I, too, can recall the strength I portrayed as my body sat high, several stories above that back porch floor. All alone, the feeling of security was overwhelming. Whether playing house with my little sister, or hiding to be all by myself, somehow this was my own special place of solitude.

As trials find their way to my grownup doorstep, sometimes I will still travel back in time to that very closet. Like sitting at the feet of Jesus, somehow that same sense of security and peace will flood over my soul. It is in the sweet presence of my Father, He graciously comforts me with the makings of His very own heavenly quilt. For each moment, each memory, and each season of my life has been fashioned by His Hands. Although not completely sewn, my Heavenly Father is carefully stitching my life as my grandmother stitched her quilts. No matter where I've been, where I am, or what's beyond the bend, God continues to sew the patchwork of my life. It is in the gathering of all of the pieces of my earthly travels to now; God is able to place them together to create His very own unique and precise design in me!

What about you? Do you have a place of serenity you can run, to find your Father? Have you seen the patchwork He has begun in your life? Take time today to sink within His arms. Take time to see how He has precisely stitched you together to be a true original design.

*"For you created my inmost being; you knit me together in my mother's*
*womb. I praise you because I am fearfully and wonderfully made;*
*your works are wonderful, I know that full well. My frame was*
*not hidden from you when I was made in the secret place."*
*Psalm 139:13, 14 & 15a (NIV)*

# THE ICEBOX

*A*s kids, going to my dad's parents home was quite a memorable adventure for my sister and me. While the adults enjoyed their time together, we spent all of our waking hours having the best of fun. From playing hide and seek in my grandparent's yard to playing cards or riding skateboards, we certainly loved spending the weekends there!

My PaPa was quite an interesting man. After my grandmother died, he was lonely without her but we were definitely not the filler we had hoped to be. Although we considered ourselves no trouble, somehow, he didn't have the same view. We were quite annoying, as far as he was concerned! He didn't intend on being mean to us, but somehow it always seemed to turn out that way. At least we thought so!

Summers in Georgia were extremely hot. Especially with the humidity! Now you know as kids, when playing has been fierce in such heat, one will thirst like never before. Unfortunately, getting a drink wasn't as easy as it seemed at my grandfather's house. Stacked neatly in his icebox were the best Double Colas you could ever drink. The trouble was getting one. It took nearly an act of congress to convince my grandfather to let go of them; especially when the kid count was more than one. Eventually, with just enough noise, a parent would come along and rescue us by convincing PaPa to let us divide those colas so the dwindled bottle count would not be so drastic.

It was not only until I became an adult that I understood the concept of stretching one's dollar. When money is tight, things seem to double in cost. Trusting in God to provide our needs becomes such a reality. Thankfully, we have a Father in Heaven who is trustworthy enough to do just that.

As our souls often run low, like those Double Colas, we can be assured that the living water is there for the taking. We can thirst no more because Christ offers us an ever-flowing stream that never runs dry.

Is your soul thirsty today? Are your needs greater than your purse? Take a trip to the ever-flowing river of life where Jesus is the giver.

> *"Let anyone who is thirsty come to me and drink.*
> *Whoever believes in me, as Scripture has said,*
> *rivers of living water will flow from within them."*
> *John 7:37(b), 38 (NIV)*

# Is It Real?

*T*here are times in our lives that we believe just because. We think things that have never been tested because we are sure there is no reason to test them. We do things, we say things and we are about things just because.

When I was young, I loved listening to the radio on road trips and just riding around town. I was intrigued and couldn't understand how so many bands could crowd into a radio station and move on and off the stage so quickly allowing the next performer his stage time. Seeing this entire scenario in my mind, however, was quickly defused. It was the day the record skipped that the light bulb came on! The wheels in my mind began to churn. What I once believed was an incredible stage show was instantly over. The truth had surfaced. The faith I had placed in the imaginary bands in my theatrical head was disbursed. The realty was at hand. My perception of the "behind the scenes" in the radio world had totally blown up. And it was devastating!

In our everyday lives, we tend to allow our perception of things to dictate our beliefs. Without question, sometimes, we just accept with no investigation. We just believe. We embrace a method. We adopt a belief and it becomes fact. It holds as truth to our inner being. Jesus specifically warns against believing without testing. He instructs His followers to "test the spirits to see if they are from God." Everything we know and believe should line up with the Word of God. Everything should shadow the image of God our Father. Even though we may believe something as silly as a live band verses a record playing, the application is apparent. The end is near. The enemy is increasingly prevalent in our day. We can't afford to be deceived, even in the little things. We must test and see, question and know, that everything is of God.

What in your life needs to be tested? What perhaps have you accepted as a fantasy, a lie or truth? Reevaluate your thought process today. Take a long look at even the simplest things that drive you. Make certain that God is God of all in your life.

*"Dear friends, do not believe every spirit, but test the spirits to see whether they are from God, because many false prophets have gone out into the world. This is how you can recognize the Spirit of God: Every spirit that acknowledges that Jesus Christ has come in the flesh is from God, but every spirit that does not acknowledge Jesus is not from God.*
*1 John 4:1(b)-3(a) (NIV)*

# FAST ASLEEP

*I* absolutely loved to spend the night at my grandparent's home in LaGrange, Georgia. Especially in the summertime! Located in a factory town, trains were constantly moving in and out of the city. I can still remember lying in that oversized bed in the back bedroom and feeling the vibration of the train's whistle. The cool summer breeze slipped through the bedroom window where my sister and I shared my grandparents' extra bed. The arrogant sound of the train's roar somehow calmed my fears while the noise gently rocked me fast to sleep. That familiar sound still speaks to my childlike heart every time I hear it, even as an adult!

Summers brought the crisp smell of sun-dried sheets, crickets singing in the evening's darkness and the dead silence of everyday life. Sleep was so fulfilling as we prepared for the day ahead. Early to bed, early to rise was always my grandparents' way of life. Most mornings, the aroma of bacon frying in her iron skillet captivated us. Homemade biscuits were a morning staple and always served and fashioned in my grandmother's very own wooden bread tray. I can still taste the sweetness of the biscuit dough that she'd slip me while my dear mother was looking the other way. Lard made those tasty biscuits last all daylong! If by chance any survived the day, they were guaranteed to be devoured at supper!

Gazing through their kitchen in my childhood mind, I can still see and taste the fresh baked peanut brittle always tucked away in my grandmother's china cabinet. Wrapped in the sweet candied smell of waxed paper, I longed for that dessert. My grandmother was absolutely the most wonderful cook whether she was preparing the first morning's meal or that anticipated afternoon snack.

Simplicity at its best and the constant perfection of daily living are sweet memories all my own. Fashioned with love, my grandparents always added that perfect touch to my childhood memory lane.

Do you possess those precious memories as a child? Are there moments of shear bliss you can recall today? Take a trip back in time. Take a trip and remember a cherished moment all your own.

*"Children's children are a crown to the aged, and parents are the pride of their children."*
*Proverbs 17:6 (NIV)*

# THE IMAGINARY LINE

*O*ften I will belly laugh when thinking of my childhood years as I was learning how to swim. At the age of eight, on numerous occasions our family gathered at the "Backwaters" with my two first cousins. (The "Backwaters" was located on Lake Harding on the Alabama, Georgia line.) My cousins were boys and they lived in Bixby, Oklahoma. We only saw them two times a year when they came for Christmas and a summer visit. They were two and four years older than my sister and me so that made them way cool cousins!

My sister and I wanted nothing more than to be as cool as them. We both listened intently when they talked about their favorite songs, television shows and activities so we could try to be like them in front of our friends. We knew our buddies would be quite impressed with us. Unfortunately trying to be cool like them was impossible! My parents would tend to quickly ruin that reputation.

When my cousins suggested that the four of us go swimming, my sister and I would sheepishly agree. For we knew mom and dad would have to come along. (They never let us go anywhere without their supervision!) While my cousins ran down the dock, splashing into the Lord-only-knows how deep lake water, the two of us were stuck on the bank suiting up our life jackets! I know we must have looked like two total nerds in our florescent orange life preservers! (I can still feel the unbelievable humiliation as I write this now!) Well, there was a swing that conveniently sat on the bank in front of our swimming area. (I know you've already guessed who sat in that swing. My dear daddy!) Yes my sister and I donned our beautiful orange life jackets, being watched by my lifeguard father and still that was not the end of it. Because of the depth of the lake, (I suppose it really was deep), dad drew an imaginary line for us to stay behind. If that weren't humiliating enough, we'd have to *walk* into the water from the bank. Yes indeed, we were utter geeks, the two of us. Thankfully though, we were only kids and my cousins would politely join us in the shallow end.

Thankfully, I know God gets a kick out of us! I can almost guarantee He laughs at me more than I care to know. Looking goofy, acting goofy or plain being goofy, God knows the real me. Even when I would prefer not to be the brunt of the laughter, He will always help me realize the good and have me laughing at myself as well!

Do you recall any funny and/or humiliating stories from your past? Take time to think of one today and belly laugh out loud. It really will do you good. By the way, has anyone ever really drowned with a life jacket in shallow water?

*"A cheerful heart is good medicine."*
*Proverbs 17:22 (NIV)*

# MY STRINGED INSTRUMENT

My third grade year marked many new opportunities. Not only did our school teach Spanish, but music was also offered as part of the curriculum. My grandmother was a pianist but no other family members were musicians. Knowing the opportunity would be a good one, my parents allowed my sister and me to join the orchestra. I played the violin and my sister played the cello.

We loved the orchestra. Rehearsals, private lessons, summer camps and school field trips allowed us to perfect our talent. One of the things I never really cared for was going to state competition. We had to stand alone in front of a panel of judges and play a number we had memorized. Site reading a song was the scariest requirements of the competition and the judges randomly chose the music. I was a nervous wreck preparing for competition and also while standing before the judges. I made myself sick worrying about having to perform and I was equally as sick afterwards worrying about how well I performed. Fortunately, I always did so much better than I ever expected!

I played the violin through elementary school and into the seventh grade. I was always second chair violin until my seventh grade year. Finally, I achieved the honor of first chair. Not only did I receive that honor, but also I was presented with a "Ritter Award." This award was given to me and one other violinist. It was the first year any students were recognized. The award was given in recognition of our excellent abilities in performance, attitude and overall accomplishments.

Playing the violin was a great accomplishment for me. Not only did it give me confidence but learning to read music opened up doors for playing the piano, guitar and singing. I am so thankful my parents allowed me to discover my gift as early as childhood! The gift of music was from God and I have continued to pursue my talent throughout my life.

God has placed special talents in each of us. He provides countless opportunities to sharpen and enhance the gifts within. Should we strive to perfect them to use as a blessing to the ones we minister to, but mostly to the one who faithfully gives of himself!

What about you? What has God gifted to you? Are you being faithful to use it for His glory? Are you purposely sharing your gift with others? Take time today to look at your life and recognize how God has equipped you. Take time to see if you need to make some adjustments in order to use what God has so graciously given to you.

*"The man who had received five bags of gold brought the other five.*
*'Master,' he said, 'You entrusted me with five bags of gold.*
*See, I have gained five more.'"*
*Matthew 25:20 (NIV)*

# WILL YOU RECOGNIZE
# THE SOUND?

*O*nce a year couldn't come soon enough for us. My babies watched it almost all of the time. Truthfully, my baby daughter watched it daily when she was five years old. Sometimes, several times a day!

When my sister and I watched it together as kids, we were glued to the television set. We began at the foot of the bed and by the ending we were glued to the head of the bed! If we could have climbed the walls, we surely would have! The story begins so normally with a girl and her dog, a very hard working family, a strange wizard and a mean old lady. That woman literally scarred my sister and me, I think, as much as she did Dorothy.

How ironic it is that the people who live in our society are so similar to characters in the storyline. As the movie progresses, the good in the story turns into uncertainty, the uncertainty into tragedy, the tragedy into eventually good. In Dorothy's journey, the mean old woman turns out to be the witch; quite fitting for her personally. The wizard is a curious one who promises things he can't ever seem to deliver. Lastly, beloved family members were there to protect her, stand beside her and keep her from harm. In the end, Dorothy comes to the realization that her unbelievable experience is only temporary. Fortunately for her, it is no more than a dream!

Like Dorothy, you and I will also face circumstances in life that can compare to, "*The Wizard of Oz*." We run into people who have no heart and seem to only be out to get us. Then we meet those that promise one thing and deliver another or simply never deliver at all. And last but not least family surrounds us and/or friends who stand beside us on our journey to protect, lead and guide us. In the grand scheme of things, we will sometimes make it through with a few bumps and bruises, and other times, the enemy will attempt to completely destroy us. We wonder if we'll ever really be able to make it through the seemingly unbearable.

One day, my friend, if you know the giver of life, you are guaranteed to find your way. No, there may be no red slippers to click together, or a balloon to soar to safety, but the mighty sound of a trumpet is guaranteed. That unmistakable sound that it's time to finally go home.

Are you going? Will you recognize the sound? Jesus is waiting for you to believe. He is standing in the midst of all of your despair ready to bear it all. Are you ready? Will you also one day say, "Oh my God, there truly is . . . .'No Place Like Home.'"

*"But in keeping with His promise we are looking forward to a new*
*Heaven and a new earth, where righteousness dwells."*
*11 Peter 3:13 (NIV)*

# HEALTH DEPARTMENT TRAUMA

*I* was raised in Roswell, Georgia and for the most part, loved the city. Many places around town held great memories for me but there was one spot I could have surely lived without! I hated going there with a passion! I will never forget turning down that very street completely aware where we were headed. To a little girl, it seemed as if we were always making the much-dreaded trip to the health department. Every time my mother grazed the very hill that led to it's front door, my sister and I would let out a bloodcurdling scream. Knowing there was no escape, I'd shake in utter fear as we sat in the waiting room. Fortunately though, the room was filled with other poor souls that, too, would be poked with a needle. (Waiting somehow eased the pain until I heard another young child scream for dear life.) My mom continually reminded us of the dreaded diseases we'd contract if we didn't go through the traumatizing horror of having that painful needle embedded in our skin. Do you really think her reasoning eased my frantic state? Heaven's no, but to have lived to be an adult of fifty-seven years, now I can say I'm glad I survived the grueling events. I'm thankful for the antidote that penetrated the jungle fever that might have surely caused my death.

There are many things in life where our humanness tends to want to run. Enviably remembering the pain of something we have endured triggers a set of emotions we must experience again. Maybe a place, a person or a thing will reflect the agonizing torment of our past experience. Fortunately, over time, we can face that fear, that experience, that trauma square in the face with determination to not allow it to control us again. Over time, with the help of God, we can defuse our fears and gracefully be the recipient of courage that shot of remembrance subsequently allowed us to achieve!

What about you? Do you, too, have a survival story from the endurance of a trial? Do you recall a memory of an unpleasant event that by chance spared your life? Thank God today for the joy of the trials we must face. Thank Him today for the possible laughter following the remembrance of your survival through the pain.

*"Consider it pure joy, my brothers and sisters, whenever you face trials of*
*many kinds, because you know that the testing of your faith produces*
*perseverance. Let perseverance finish its work so that you may*
*be mature and complete, not lacking anything."*
*James 1:2-4 (NIV)*

# HIS SOOTHING VOICE

*B*eing raised a Georgia girl, it was understandable I'd also be raised to love baseball. The Atlanta Braves were of course the favorite in our household! One of my only real memories with my mother's father was going to Turner Field in Atlanta to see the Braves play. I loved it!

Even a more distinct memory of mine was listening to the games on the portable radio at my other grandfather's house. Traveling to LaGrange, Georgia, my family often stayed the weekends at my PaPa's house, my father's daddy. Summer evenings there was one of my most vivid memories. The bedroom next to the swing on the front porch was where my sister, my two cousins and I always slept. Positioned on a homemade pallet on the hardwood floor, we slept on top of several homemade quilts and a cool white sheet on top. Because of the heat and no air conditioner, the windows were always raised. On the porch sat my PaPa. Every evening, he would plug up his portable radio and place it in the window of our bedroom. Sitting in the porch swing, where he could capture the breeze, he would swing for hours listening to the ballgame. Yes, the game was good but more than that was the faint sound of the swing creaking back and forth and the announcer's soothing voice. It put us all to sleep in no time! To this day, I can still quiet my soul if I close my eyes and go back to those nights there in my grandfather's home. There is nothing more comforting than a place that can sweetly soothe your being. Past or present, you can always go to that place in your mind!

I still love the Atlanta Braves to this day. Going home in the summertime to Georgia, I always know my daddy will have the TV tuned into the baseball game. Although he's not on his porch listening to his radio, the sound of the announcers resonates throughout the house. It instantly takes me back to childhood. There is a calm feeling that comes over me as I remember those nights long ago on my grandfather's front bedroom floor.

God, too, has a way of soothing our souls with the comforting words we find in His Word. Calming our fears, soothing our hurts, guiding our hearts and leading our paths are some of the many ways He moves us. Leaning on Him to give us wisdom to make decisions and knowledge to know which way to move forward, comes from the promises in His Word. The key is finding that place of calm, peaceful solitude to allow ourselves to hear what He wants to tell us. Lying still in His presence while He ministers to our souls brings healing, understanding and much needed rest.

What about you? When was the last time you laid before the Lord in His presence? When have you allowed Him to speak to your soul through His instructive Word? Take time today to bask in your Father's presence. Take time to hear His soothing voice.

*"For everything that was written in the past was written to teach*
*us, so that through the endurance taught in the Scriptures*
*and the encouragement they provide we might have hope."*
*Romans 15:4 (NIV)*

# CAN YOU SEE THEM?

*I*n 1970, I was a young girl of twelve years old. Being raised in church, I totally believed in Jesus and I knew that death meant meeting my Savior face to face. In this same year, death presented itself to many of my immediate family members. My father's mother was one of those.

My daddy's momma was a wonderful woman. She was the type of grandmother grandkids loved. I still remember her smile. She seemed to always be in the kitchen and her cooking was everyone's favorite! Often when we'd visit, she would let me stand next to her and watch her make her incredible homemade biscuits. The memory of her wooden biscuit tray will always be etched in my mind. Although my mom was not a fan of my sister and I having biscuit dough, my grandmother always slipped us a pinch of some to eat while she made her signature biscuits. As crazy as it sounds, they were even delicious uncooked!

Suffering from emphysema and other health issues, my grandmother was hospitalized in March of 1970. My daddy and his four sisters were there. My father was her baby so he stayed with her every moment of her hospital stay. Just before the end, she called my daddy's name. "What is it momma?" my daddy said. "Do you see them Bobby?" she asked. "What momma? See what?" "The angels Bobby. They are here to take me home." Although he never saw them, He believed. He believed because his momma saw.

I love to hear my daddy tell me this story. I too believed without a doubt but God confirmed, with my own grandmother, that there are truly angels. In my grandmother's "home-going," the Lord saw fit that she share with her son the shear comfort of knowing that she would not be alone. Like royalty, my grandmother was escorted into the presence of her almighty God!

Neither my father nor I may ever see the presence of angels ourselves, but we know that his momma did. What a moment. What a memory. What a mighty God we serve!

What about you? Are there moments God has proven Himself to you? Are there times and places He has taken you or shown you proving to be the God we serve? Take time today to bask in His presence. Take time today to remember and know that He is who He says He is. He is *The Great I Am"*

*"I, Jesus, have sent my angel to give you this testimony for the churches. I am*
*the Root and the Offspring of David, and the bright Morning Star."*
*Revelation 22:16 (NIV)*

# My Entangled Heart

The day was a difficult one. My stomach churned and the emotions beginning to surface were none I'd really ever experienced. I walked into that church along side of my sister and my two favorite cousins. I knew in their presence, I'd have to control my surfacing emotions.

Standing in wait, we began the slow processional to our pre-appointed places. My seat was on the left side of the sanctuary. It was when we finally all sat down, that the music stopped. The only real sound at that point was an occasional whimper or a sniffle from the crowd. Even the pastor's footsteps seemed to echo as he approached the podium.

"Today is a sad day. . .but a happy one as well," the preacher said. How on earth could he say anything about being happy at a time like this I thought? As he continued though, I realized the joy of which he was speaking. My grandmother's suffering had finally ended. Her soul was with her maker and her earthly body was soon to be buried in wait of Jesus' return.

The longer I sat, the more I hurt. The sobs from her children seemed to only irritate my deepest emotions. My tears seemed uncontrollable. The ache of my heart was like nothing I'd ever felt before. Finally, I had an idea. If I pinched myself, I'd distract my emotions. The pain from my self-infliction would side track my waterfall of tears. Without delay, I did it. It worked! The tears stopped. For a moment, the funeral, my hurt and my presence in that church disappeared. My concentration was strictly on the pinching instead of what was happening around me.

How often do we pinch ourselves in order to distract from the reality of life? How often do we avoid a situation at all costs? We tip toe around as if it isn't even happening. God tells us that He will be there in the midst of our troubles. He wants to be our guide, our comforter, and our friend.

Is there a situation you need to allow Him to control? Are there situations you need to face? Allow God to walk beside you. Allow your Father to be your strength as well as your guide.

*"Such a high priest truly meets our need – one who is holy, blameless,*
*pure, set apart from sinners, exalted above the heavens*
*Hebrews 7:26 (NIV)*

# THE BROKEN GLASS

My childhood days with my sister were great! We loved playing together and doing things that made our time not so boring. Sometimes, however, our creative minds brought visions of the most adventurous days! Many times, however, our parents didn't quite agree with our ideas! Insistent on doing things 'our way', we didn't always obey and follow instructions as we were told!

One afternoon with complete and purposeful disobedience, I proceeded with sheer determination to do things my way. My mom was leaving us home alone while she ran into town and before leaving she warned us not to add hot water to our stone cold pool water in the back yard. Knowing the water was way too cold for the two of us to swim, we did it anyway, our way!

As soon as my mom drove away, my sister and I ran inside and filled huge glass jars that held the perfect amount of hot water. That warm water was the exact ingredient we needed to warm that freezing pool water. Filling and pouring, filling and pouring, back and forth we ran, until the water had reached the perfect temperature!

Unpredictably, the excess water that spilled from the many trips back and forth to the kitchen covered the outside of my sister's jug caused her hands to slip. As she lost her grip, the jar fell, crashing on to the concrete and slicing her pinky finger almost to the bone! The blood trickling down her finger was immediate evidence of the reason why mom had warned us. Our strong desire to swim caused our unwilling, rebellious behavior and drove us on to disobedience.

Knowing my contribution, but no evidence seen on me, I pretended for years that I had nothing to do with her accident. It was not until I was in my thirty's that I finally came clean with the truth. My conscience finally got the best of me, and knowing I could not be corrected or punished as an adult, I 'fessed up'. It's funny though, how that single lie followed me all of those years.

Both of my siblings continually taunted me as they tagged me with that tale. Although the truth would have earned a spanking, the odds are it would have remained forgotten. Instead, it crept up for years in family conversations. Knowing my guilt, I always had to lie over and over again. Today, I'm thankful to be set free from that haunting past. Though it may be funny now, it took years to see any humor from my side of the fence.

What is it today you've chosen not to face? What is it you are quietly allowing another to take the blame? Allow the Savior to cleanse your past. Allow the Father to breathe within a fresh breath of relief, guilt free.

*"So I strive always to keep my conscience clear before God and man."*
*Acts 24:16 (NIV)*

# OUR TUMBLING TALENTS

My seventh grade year offered an opportunity to do something I had always wanted to do. Tumbling classes took place after school and not only my sister and I, but my cousin got to learn the art of gymnastics. We all three loved to learn together! We picked up quickly all the stunts and I must say we were quite good. We, fortunately, had discovered a new talent in our childhood days. My personal favorite was to stand on my head. In fact, if the blood had not stored up and caused a headache, I probably would have stayed on it! My sister, however, simply loved to tumble.

One day, the three of us arranged a sleepover at our house. Being a little mischievous, my sister decided to show off her newfound talent of tumbling. Completely ignoring the constant reminder my mother often gave, she began to exercise her talents disobediently on the family couch. As she continued to tumble over and over again, the wall became her resting place. Without warning, her entire leg found itself engaged within the sheetrock. Oh yes. The hole was huge! Not only did we fear for our lives, we were quickly reminded that my parents had just put the house on the market to sell! Instantly, we positioned a pillow to camouflage the evidence. As you might imagine, the hole was discovered, our talents detained to the floor, and our slumber party was immediately cancelled!

Today I laugh at the choices we made that day. Yes, we were only being kids, but we learned a valuable lesson! It wasn't enough for us to simply obey. We wanted to do things our way. We failed to even imagine that our parents were wise enough to have predicted that very outcome. Monkey business on any of the furniture was strictly prohibited! It was in our disobedience that we found out exactly why we should have refrained.

What about you? What is God telling you not to do? What is it you insist on finding out all on your own anyway? Ask God today to help if you have not listened in the past. Ask Him to help you be obedient to His words of wisdom. Ask Him to guide you away from the middle of a mess you could have easily avoided.

*"Children, obey your parents in everything, for this pleases the Lord."*
*Colossians 3:20 (NIV)*

# COUSINS

ousins. . . We were the greatest of friends! Even though we were probably twenty-fifth cousins, twice removed, you would have thought we were really first! My sister and I were so proud to be related to one particular cousin that it didn't even matter how. We would do just about anything to get to spend time with her. I can remember agreeing to clean the kitchen, clean the toilets, or whatever my mother needed so the three of us could get together.

One weekend my Cousin had a birthday party at her house. It was a slumber party with at least eight of her closest friends. We had a great time watching television, playing games, talking, eating and finally falling asleep in the wee hours of the morning. My sister was the early morning riser of the bunch. It really did not matter how late she went to bed, she 'rose with the roosters!' This party was no different! That morning, just as she had done at all of our other slumber nights, she was up and ready to go! While the rest of us slept, my sister enjoyed chatting with my cousin's mom. The thing we did not know was that she was telling our cousin's mother all of our secrets! Just enjoying the time together, she didn't think twice about sharing our private information. Finally, after much investigation, we figured out who the snitch was among us! From then on, we were furious at her. So furious that we agreed to disband the three amigos while regrouping as two, minus my sister! Actually, I have found sisters usually do much better if they have separate friends anyway.

Today I marvel at our past. My sister has gone on to be with the Lord, but our childhood memories will never die! My cousin and I have spent many hours reminiscing of the days of 'ole. The moments of laughter, adventure, and incredible fun were all our own. Using our imagination and creative skills, we painted a beautiful mental picture of our days that will last a lifetime! I thank God for my family. I thank Him for my precious sister and the treasured times we shared. Although incomplete without her, I can view a rerun of our times in my mind forever.

What about you? Are there memories in your days gone by? Can you giggle and laugh about the childhood tales you've stored up? Spend time today thanking God for the sweet memories and sweet moments of the family He purposely chose for you!

*"Satisfy us in the morning with your unfailing love,*
*that we may sing for joy and be glad all our days."*
*Psalm 90:14 (NIV)*

# THE PERFECT INVENTION

*I* grew up with a father who should be a millionaire today. Out of just about anything, he could make everything, and not one thing was patented.

Summers were very hot in Georgia and the humidity made the temperature seem as if we lived slap dab in the middle of the desert. Well, my daddy would listen to my sister and I whine enough about the heat that his inventive mind would churn. One day, we walked outside to find our own three-foot pool. Now this pool was not your normal in ground, or even a plastic one from the local dime store. Today, it would be referred to as an above ground pool. In the back of his old Ford green truck, he had laid down as a foundation, a thick piece of plastic. On top of that, his one and only brown tarp draped over the sides of that old truck. Inside, he had filled that baby up with cool water and it was the most awesome swimming pool my eyes had ever seen. Now I'm here to tell you that was the life and it didn't even leak!

My sister and I swam for days in that homemade pool. Little did I know until adulthood, that my concerned momma graciously added a little dab of Clorox bleach to kill any germs. She didn't want her little darlings to be sick! Unaware, we swam and swam having no clue of anything but the sheer enjoyment of our new pool! It was indeed the greatest place on earth. I suppose the germs did die. Thankfully, my sister and I didn't!

When I think about the fun we had in that old Ford truck, I know my daddy must have been proud. That truck was definitely what Oprah refers to today as "multi-purpose." My sister and I didn't care because that heat was quickly sweltered by the delight of my father's perfect invention!

I wonder if Jesus, too, had fun like we did as kids. I wonder if He, too, trusted His Father to provide all of His needs even when it came to fun? Now that I think about it, I wonder if the Sea of Galilee really had plastic and a tarp under it?

What is it that your parents provided you as a child that Jesus, too, may have enjoyed? Take time today to ponder into the joy of your childhood past.

*"I am not saying this because I am in need, for I have learned to be content whatever the circumstances. I know what it is to be in need, and I know what it is to have plenty.*
*I have learned the secret of being content in any and every situation,*
*whether well fed or hungry, whether living in plenty or in want.*
*I can do all this through him who gives me strength."*
*Philippians 4: 11-13 (NIV)*

# WE HAD TO SHARE

Growing up, my sister and I were two years apart. We didn't know life without the other. One of the things I remember most about our childhood was having to share everything. We shared a bedroom, clothes, shoes, toys and most anything else you could think of to share. That word was a "must" in our household! Now, we did have those special things that we claimed as our own. Things that had our names engraved on them and things we received as gifts from family and or friends were ours alone. They were off limits to the other!

Most of the time we were both OK with sharing. And then there were those few times we were not! We wanted to experience single ownership. We wanted to call stuff "mine!" Frankly stated, we wanted to rebel against the rule. We wanted to say NO to being bound by the chains of sharing with the other! Unfortunately, we didn't usually win out over the rule. It was permanent!

One of the things I remember sharing was our food. It was a given. I always figured it was because we didn't eat a lot so to prevent wasting what "*the kids in Africa*" couldn't have, we just ate what the other didn't. Once I became a teenager and my appetite increased, I realized that wasn't really all of it. My mom and dad were penny pinchers. They were excellent savers. They knew that in order to have, you needed to use wisdom to prevent wasting. I have to admit there was very little left over at our dinner table. We were full and so was their bank account! Watching what you spend and taking advantage of coupons, sales and rationing will guarantee money back in your pocket!

Whether you have to share with a sibling, a partner or a spouse, sharing is a good thing. It teaches us the importance of respecting what we have. God created us to give of ourselves as He has so given to us. Often, we miss that. In our selfish human nature, all we want is to have our own things. . .our own possessions. We forget that in following Him, we often have to sacrifice the things to which we lay too much claim. Many times in scripture the Lord asked people to leave everything to follow Him. He wanted all of their hearts and not their stuff. That's a tough one when we can so easily get attached to what we have and what we have earned. The best part is, when we choose to freely give all that we have, with no strings attached, God is faithful to return to us so much more than we ever dreamed or imagined.

What is it today that you have had to share? Have you done it with joy or been forced to give what you would have rather kept to yourself? Take time today to evaluate your present circumstances. Take time to ask God what He would have you share with another. More importantly, ask Him what He would have you give up completely!

*"No one should seek their own good, but the good of others."*
*1 Corinthians 10:24 (NIV)*

# ELVIS TO THE RESCUE

*I*t's funny how adolescents seek to continually find things to do to rid themselves of "the parents". My sister and I were no exceptions to that rule. In fact, we couldn't wait to be excused from them, especially when we went to visit my cousins at my grandparent's home in LaGrange, Georgia. Wanting to grow up and have a little freedom is certainly a natural thing, isn't it?

Summers always allowed our cousins and us to venture out into the city, just the four of us. Downtown was the LaGrange Theatre. The daytime matinees were excellent opportunities for the cousins to at least pretend we were all grown up! Most of the time we were the only ones in the theatre. It didn't matter to us what was playing or who was there just as long as the air conditioner could cool us off and we were officially parent-free!

One of the most memorable things about going to the theatre was getting to see Elvis Presley movies. He was the ***King of Rock and Roll*** then and now! Sitting in that movie show watching that "*Hunka Hunka Burnin Love*" was a memory I never knew I wouldn't forget. Seeing his manly, creative moves certainly made a young girl like me wonder! Wanting to grow up and being caught in between being a young girl and adulthood was an awkward place to be. Eventually though, it happened. Certainly not without the vivid etching of that gorgeous dark-headed man engraved in my memory!

Life is filled with adventures, people, places and things that captivate and leave marks on our memories. Some good. Some bad. Nevertheless, they leave an impression. The great thing is we most often have a choice on what we partake in that deposits it's remnants in our thinking and video minds. It is the wellspring of our life. Although we'd like to venture off on our own, like children from their parents, most often staying within the boundaries of discipline and wholeness is vital to create a healthy wellbeing.

What about you? Have you chosen to stay within the boundaries of the Word of God? Have you made a conscience effort to remain faithful to fill up with great memories and moments from the past? Ask God today how you can transform your mind and remain in His Word. Ask Him today what you can do to continually stay faithful and filled with His goodness and love, and continually create sweet memories of days gone by.

> "*A good man brings good things out of the good stored up in his heart, and an evil man brings evil things out of the evil stored up in his heart. For the mouth speaks what the heart is full of.*"
> Luke 6:45 (NIV)

# OUR HOLIDAY TRADITIONS

Our family tradition began for my sister and I in the 1960's. Every year on Thanksgiving night, our family watched television to see the lighting of the famous Christmas tree. The tree was located at Rich's Department Store in downtown Atlanta, Georgia. One year, I remember specifically going to Rich's to witness the lighting in person. There were thousands of other Georgians that showed up to view the sight with us.

Every holiday, mom and dad set aside a Saturday in December that was specifically dedicated to spending the day with family in downtown Atlanta. The first stop was for lunch at the world famous "Krystal." I can still remember sitting on the silver stools while watching the grillers prepare our "little" hamburgers. Those hamburgers were literally almost bite-size but the best I'd ever put in my mouth!

Next, we drove to **Rich's Department Store** to ride the "**Pink Pig**." This was truly the highlight of the season. Standing in line with hundreds of other adults and youngsters, we climbed the ramp to the roof of the department store. Reaching the end of the line, my sister, dad and I were positioned in our seats while the "**Pink Pig**" train attendant closed the pig's doors. Finally, the train began its journey around the entire roof of the store. Looking below were Santa's reindeer. Up ahead was the huge Christmas tree that we had seen light up from our living room's television. I will never forget the ornaments that hung on that huge tree. They were as big as me I believe! Finally at the end of the ride, the train took us over the side of the building overlooking downtown Atlanta. It was an amazing sight. Captured in my childhood mind forever, are the many special memories my family and I created those many years ago.

Our entire lives are filled with memorable moments from places, times, events and people. Each of them mark past those vary journeys we've traveled. Each of them creates a picture in our minds that we never forget and love to share with others.

God can also relate to special times as He sent His son to walk the earth for you and me. Marking His journey in His Word, the story can be recalled by all who read it. Miracles, moments and memories are shared with the reader. The most incredible story is the birth of His Son, Jesus. The birth of a Savior. The birth of the one that gave His life to save our own.

What about you? Have you a memory that's like no other? Do you believe in a Savior that saved the world? Take time today to spend it with the one that came just for you. Take time today to remember the God who walks with you in all of your memorable moments.

*"I praise you for remembering me in everything and for holding to the*
*traditions just as I passed them on to you."*
*1 Corinthians 11:2 (NIV)*

# A COMMON CAUSE

*M*y seventh grade year was at Roswell Elementary School in Roswell, Georgia. Like most schools, even back then fundraisers were a must. Twice yearly, our school chose to have a paper drive. In the front parking lot, wooden stick signs marked with every grade from first to seventh, lined the length of the school. For one week, students from every grade went to neighbors, friends, family and even strangers soliciting their old newspapers. Over a period of time, people saved and waited for the same class representative to come and retrieve their stack of papers.

My mom and dad were the best fundraiser parents ever! While my daddy drove his old Ford truck, my mom knocked on every door and called everyone she knew to go pick up their papers. From far and wide they trotted. As the week progressed, everyday those newspapers grew in numbers. The object of the fundraiser was the class that produced the most papers won the contest. The prize was simply being known as the winner, the best! Afterwards, the papers were taken to a local recycling plant in exchange for money for the school. Every year, my class won!

During each event, people in the community worked along side of the youth to support not only the school but also the students. Relationships were made, kids were challenged with a much-needed cause and a difference was consequently made. My parents were always a part of the effort. They showed us how to succeed at anything, even if it was just a paper drive. All in all, the community got rid of their papers, kids worked together for a common cause and the school was rewarded with the funds it so desperately needed.

God does the same with our lives. The cause is for Christ. The mission is humanity. God supports our efforts and joins us as brothers and sisters for one great commission. Ultimately, the winners of the prize are the ones who choose life, the ones who accept the giver of life as their own.

Take time today to know with certainty that you are on the winning team. Thank God today for leading you to the prize of your eternal heavenly home!

*"I press on toward the goal to win the prize for which*
*God has called me heavenward in Christ Jesus."*
*Philippians 3:14 (NIV)*

# WITH DILIGENCE

My grandmother lived across the street from the Roswell United Methodist Church in Roswell, Georgia. She, my grandfather, great grandmother, aunt and our family were all members there. My grandmother was a woman of excellence. Whatever she did, she did it with fervor and diligence.

As a volunteer at the church, I remember her being the president of the altar guild. Her job was to prepare the communion trays every time communion was served. Laid on her kitchen counter were several hundred tiny glass cups that she filled with grape juice for every service. Once the communion service was complete, she would bring all of those cups back to her house. The thing I remember most about this task was her diligence. She would stand at her kitchen sink for hours. She washed each individual glass cup. Not only did she wash them, but also she made sure every one was dried to perfection. Holding each one up to the light she made certain no spot of any kind remained on any part of each glass.

My grandmother, like God does with us, took pride in her position. She knew what she was doing was more than just washing and spotlessly drying cups and loved it. She knew what it took to make those seemingly just glass cups, become useful instruments in the remembrance of the shed blood on the cross at Calvary. Although our lives may look like not much at all, God sees our potential. He will work diligently to wash us, dry us off, and use us as instruments to glorify who He is and what He's done for us all. God will carefully fill us up with Himself and pour us out to the world in uniquely different ways.

How is God using you today? Perhaps He is in the process of cleaning you up so He can fill you up? Maybe He is pouring you out. Wherever you are in the process of being used, God is working. He is diligently making sure who you are and what you do for His kingdom is making a difference. Take time today to thank Him for choosing you. Thank Him also for His willingness to make you into the instrument He has created you to be.

*"Yet you, Lord, are our Father. We are the clay, you are the*
*potter; we are all the work of your hand."*
*Isaiah 64:8 (NIV)*

# Young Adulthood

# DREAMS DO COME TRUE

*I* was a seventh grader when I discovered one of my talents. I could sing. I loved to sing. Continuing into college, I finally settled in on the pursuit of becoming a Vocal Performance major.

Once I started college, from sun up to sun down, I sang. I joined choirs, girl's ensemble, took voice lessons and was chosen for a second soprano position in the campus pop group called, *Daybreak*. I was living the dream and loved every minute of it!

Winter break, both my freshman and sophomore years, our pop group went on tour. For ten days we traveled from Georgia to Florida performing for churches and schools all over the region. From pop songs to four-part harmonies, we sang our hearts out. We performed in basement fellowship halls of churches to auditoriums with nearly an audience of 1,000 students.

As a shy girl for most of my years, I became someone I longed to be. I became empowered. I became self-assured in that I could do something good. In the process of it all, I discovered that there was just something about that stage. The stage was more than a platform. It was an instrument of empowerment for me. It was a place of confidence I had sought my entire life. It's even hard to express in words the confidence that captivated me in those moments that I performed. Fearlessly singing solo, my brave voice echoed in the silence of every tamed audience. I can still recall standing in pronounced assurance. Suddenly, hearing the roaring claps of the surprised and satisfied audience, created within me the boost of confidence I had always needed. That assurance was the reality of making my unbelievable dreams become reality!

As *Daybreak* toured the many schools and churches, meeting our audiences was an incredible moment as well. Often, people would present a program from our performance schedule and ask the vocalists to sign them. I was no exception. That was a dream come true in itself! As a little girl, I had often practiced my handwriting. Within the dreams of my childhood mind I had dreamed of becoming a star. I had dreamed of signing autographs and being known by many.

Many may not know me today but the one that matters the most, my Savior, Jesus Christ, knows me! He knows me well. He loves me and has equipped me with gifts and talents so that He may use me for His glory! Equipped with His strength and boldness, I am empowered to do all that He has called me to accomplish. Pronouncing His love, grace and mercy He has prepared the stage for me. I am living out His perfect plan for me.

What about you? Has Christ equipped you with a calling on your life? Have you allowed Him to use you for His glory? Take time today to marvel in your uniqueness. Take time to ask what God has purposed you to do for the glory of His Kingdom!

*"Being confident of this, that He who began a good work in you will carry it on to completion until the day of Christ Jesus."*
*Philippians 1:6 (NIV)*

# CAMP GLISSON

*M*y teen years began to stir up new emotion as God's Spirit came into my life. Accepting Christ as my Savior at the age of thirteen changed my life. I began to crave the things of God. Being very involved in my church's youth group, various activities deepened my relationship and desire to serve God. One of the events I always anticipated was the adventure of our quarterly youth retreats. My heart often ached for that closeness with God. I knew I could always find my Father's beauty and His presence at Camp Glisson!

Camp Glisson was nestled in the hills of Dahlonega, Georgia. It was an incredibly beautiful retreat spot. Twice a year our youth group spent a weekend there. Retreating away with God not only increased our commitment to Him, but it strengthened friendships with other Christians alike! Even though we were given several opportunities for free time throughout the weekend's agenda, I found myself not so prone to want to participate. Instead, God would inevitably draw me near to His glory at one particular place on that property. "*The Falls*," had to be the most incredible piece of evidence of His majesty I had ever seen. The constant sound of the rushing water, pouring over a massive collection of rocks, would almost take my breath away. Many times I would climb up the side of the falls to the top in the wooded area that invited nearly every soul. Being at the top allowed even the simple man the ability to see the grandeur of His work!

One day in particular, as I climbed, I noticed two trees formed together with a stretched out place for one to lie. Accepting the invitation, I obediently positioned myself between the limbs. With pen and paper in hand, God and I would together sit among the constant sound of flowing water. My teacher and guide dictated the lesson as I took note of the words He spoke to me. Forever etched in my mind, that day has been a constant reminder of the great love my Heavenly Father has for me.

As Moses drew near to God, after hiking the road to Mount Sinai, I had also reached my mountain. Although my face may not have been radiant when I returned, my heart certainly was. Those moments, in His presence, were transforming to my teenage life. My heart and mind will be forever captivated by the time He spent with me that day.

Today, your Mt. Sinai is, to, close at hand. Seek out a place, begin the climb and know that God is anticipating your arrival. Take time today to follow with heartfelt obedience and bask in His divine presence, just you and your Creator!

> *"When Moses came down from Mount Sinai with the two tablets of the*
> *covenant law in his hands, he was not aware that his face*
> *was radiant because he had spoken with the Lord!"*
> *Exodus 34:29 (NIV)*

# Recycling The Rolls

*I*n the ninth grade, my parents moved our family from our home where I attended first through eighth grade. The new house was located in a different county so my sister and I had to change schools. Besides a new school, we had to make new friends, find a new church and work on rebuilding what we lost.

Fortunately the church we fell in love with gave us all we needed! Joining the youth group provided a new family and us with amazing friends. My parents also joined the youth serving as counselors.

Deepening relationships meant spending lots of time together. Sleepovers, Bible Studies, retreats and special events brought many of the teens to my parent's house. There was rarely a dull moment! Although we were well-behaved youth, occasionally there had to be a bit of mischief thrown into the mix. In fact, until this day, we still have no true confessors. The truth is, we probably never will.

Those 'interesting events' seemed to occur at our house quite frequently. When the sunshine rose on our front yard, many mornings were brighter than others. The brighter mornings were due to the white that covered our trees and lawn. And when that covering occurred, there was lots of it! Toilet paper, I mean. Yes, rolls and rolls were scattered on our property. Strange to most, my mom loved it! You ask why? Well, she saw a blessing in it. Every rolling occurrence provided unused rolls of toilet paper that did not totally unroll. Every time, she scouted out those rolls with a vengeance. They were like gold to her. She saved them every one and guess what? We got to use them! Yes, she didn't have to buy toilet paper for a very long time! When the stash pile got low, she'd announce it was time for another evening surprise visit! Needless to say, my sister and I were mortified at her behavior. Fortunately, the other youth did not blame us for my mother's ridiculous obsession!

Life will often cover us with unexpected happenings. Heartache, pain, misfortunes and other unpredictable mishaps will come our way. Although the way doesn't seem easy, if we look beyond the mess, we can find the joy in it. If we look past the evident and focus on the blessing, we can easily see the end of the pain.

What about you? Are you looking at a mess? Where is your focus? Are you blinded by the light or seeking the source of the light? Take time today to refocus your lens and recapture the true beauty in your view.

*"But seek first His kingdom and His righteousness, and all these things will*
*be given to you as well. Therefore do not worry about tomorrow, for*
*tomorrow will worry about itself. Each day has enough trouble of its own"*
*Matthew 6:33 &34 (NIV)*

# COULDN'T LET GO

*I*n the summer of 1977, I met my husband. I had just graduated from high school and this was his senior year. For years, I had prepared to go to college. A career and moving on with my life was a given. Once I met my boyfriend though, a wrench was put into my plan.

I was a vocalist and a violinist. I played in the orchestra from third to eighth grade and loved it! I moved to a new school in ninth grade and was forced to concentrate just on my voice, as the new school system did not teach stringed instruments.

In my senior year, I received a four-year scholarship to Columbus College in Columbus, GA. My major was to be music and I would be a member of the orchestra. I was a little nervous never being away from home. The worst thing was I now had a boyfriend. After giving me a promise ring in the summer, I began to have second thoughts. My whole life I prayed for the man of my dreams, I knew I had found him and did not want to leave him.

We discussed my departure and the closer the time came to leave, the more unsure I became. The day before I left, he told me that if we were going to be five hours away, he would probably start dating other girls. My heart fell like a ton of bricks. I could not possibly allow this to happen. No one was going to take my prince charming! After some soul searching and master planning, I knew what I had to do.

With the car loaded down, the next morning my parents and my boyfriend drove with me to my new school. Driving my car, I knew I would have transportation to return home when I needed to. Finally arriving in Columbus, I unpacked my bags and tried to act grown-up. I said good-bye to my family.

After only two hours, I realized I knew in my heart what I really wanted. Repacking my car and explaining to the house owners, I quickly headed back home. I gave up my four-year scholarship and I returned to the one with whom I wanted to spend the rest of my life. He, too, was grateful for my decision. My parents, on the other hand, were not so receptive but decided to work with me. I enrolled in a college near by and my boyfriend and I have been husband and wife for 37 years. It was the best decision I have ever made!

What about you? Has God placed someone or something in your life that you know is meant to be? Have you had to make a decision based on God's will for you and not man's no matter how good it looked? Take time today to thank the Lord for giving you the wisdom to know what is best. Thank Him today for walking beside you even when the walk is not the one others may choose for you. In the end your happiness and your decisions are blessed when they are truly God's will for your life!

*"Blessed are those who keep His statutes and seek Him with all*
*their heart – they do no wrong but follow His ways.*
*Psalm 119:2-3 (NIV)*

# THE FAMILY MANSION

My grandmother's home was located in Historic Roswell, Georgia. It was positioned right across the street from the First United Methodist Church on Mimosa Boulevard. Her home was rich with history. In my teenage years, it was over 100 years old. I loved it when she let my sister and me spend the night. In our eyes, the house was a mansion! The rooms had twelve-foot ceilings and all the floors were hardwood. I especially loved to take a bath there. She had an antique bear claw tub! I will never forget relaxing in it like I was a true princess!

The basement was kind of creepy to me. It had dirt floors and was always so dark. Originally, this area of the house was one previous owner's slave quarters. One room served as the kitchen. I will never forget carved into the wall of that Georgia clay was a homemade fire pit. Bricks were placed within the clay securing their cooking area. A big black pot, hung from the center of the hole. My grandmother never really told me any specific stories, but whenever I walked in those rooms, I could sense the history made there.

Her house also had an upstairs. The wooden staircase was extremely wide and elegant! My grandmother never used this part of the house though. In fact, a large plank of wood had been placed there to block off the area. Sometimes, I talked my grandmother into taking my sister and I upstairs so we could just look around. I loved the rooms. All of them were A-framed shaped and had floor to ceiling length windows. My sister and I pretended we lived there. I always tried to convince my grandmother and my mother that we needed an official room up there.

I can still visualize in my mind every inch of this house. The rooms did not have light switches but buttons that you pushed to turn the lights on. Every room included its' own fireplace as well. All with closets, the rooms had three feet of divided space that served as entryways into each room. Curtains were placed on each side of the divided spaces so as not to see through to the other side. Those were our most favored hiding spots!

My grandmother eventually sold her home and moved into a newer one. Although my grandmother has passed on the memories of the old homestead and the amazing stories she shared with us are some of my most cherished memories.

What about you? Is there a place in your past that you cherish? Are their incredible memories that represent your childhood? Take time today to look back in time and thank God for the blessings He has bestowed upon you. Take time to thank Him for the family He so kindly named your own!

*"'From one man He made all the nations, that they should inhabit*
*the whole earth; and He marked out their appointed times in*
*history and the boundaries of their lands."*
*Acts 17:26 (NIV)*

# MEMORIES FOR A LIFETIME

eaving home and moving to college was a huge step for this home girl. I was very dependent on my parents and siblings until the day I left. With a new boyfriend and the reality of making a life for myself, I adjusted as best I could. Growing up and moving on was a given!

Being a people person, moving into a dorm with hundreds of other girls was right up my alley. I quickly made great friends. Hanging out, sharing our stories, studying with classmates and joining a sorority made way for a whole new life for me.

My second year of lodging was in a suite of eight girls. My new roommate was my best friend. We met our first year. Our suite was made up of girls that had not known one another until they met in college. It was a great mix of girls. We had so much fun together! My roommate and I, however, were the ones that stirred up all the fun and memory making. I must also admit, I was the darer. My roomie loved to be dared.

Dressing up like the Easter bunny, we had the girls place Easter baskets outside their doors so we could fill them with candy. At Christmas time, we decorated the dorm suite and exchanged gifts along with a great party. Any time we could think of something to celebrate, we did. Any time we could play a joke on another, we did. Sneaking boys in, panty raids, prank phone calls and keeping our suite mates up at night were just a few of our days of fun.

Unlike high school, in college you live with your friends and it can either make you or break you. To this day my roommate is one of my best friends. She and I have always been there for one another even though we live miles and miles apart. We have witnessed each other's weddings, births, job transfers, kid troubles, family troubles and even death. For a lifetime, we will be sisters, sisters until the end!

Fortunately when my college days came to an end my friendships did not. Although we all have different careers, lives and families, we still treasure the years we spent in our suite together. The laughter, the tears, the talks, the stories and the memories will always remain. Our hearts were transformed when we met one another! These friends forever changed me!

God has created us for relationships. He knows how important communication with others and friendships will be as we walk out the story of our lives. Take time today to communicate with your Father. Thank Him for the friends He has so graciously sent your way. Thank Him also for being the best friend you will ever hope to have.

*"May the Lord our God be with us as He was with our*
*ancestors; May He never leave us nor forsake us."*
*1 Kings 8:57 (NIV)*

# MY NUMBER ONE FAN

*M*y college years were two of the most rewarding in my life. Being a music major allowed me to truly perfect the natural talent God had given me. Not only was I in the college choir, but the girl's ensemble and the select choir. The year also permitted me to be a member of the first year pop group, "Daybreak." The group consisted of eight voices. I was also a soloist.

Every Wednesday on campus convocation was held. From week to week the speakers changed. One particular Wednesday, "Daybreak" was invited to perform. We gladly accepted!

My sister was also a student at the college. Most of our lives we both participated in extra circular activities together. We were very different in many ways but we both loved music. However, a singer, she was not! Being the oldest, I always seemed to mother her. She never took things near as seriously as I did. I was very emotional and she was very stubborn showing very little emotion.

When "Daybreak" sang that week, I could see my sister from the stage. She sat in the very back. When the group completed their show set, it was time for me to take the stage. My solo number was a surprise for her. Favoring the ever-popular Barbara Streisand, I choose one of her numbers from her movie hit, "*A Star Is Born*". I looked like her and I sounded like her. As I sang, I could see the amazement in not only the audience's eyes, but also my sister's. Concluding my performance of the hit, "*Woman In The Moon*", I received a standing ovation. Although overwhelmed with excitement that I had pleased the crowd, the one thing that touched me more was my sister. From the back, I could see her on her feet clapping madly along with the audience. Not only was she applauding my performance, but she was crying. Tears were streaming down her face. Her approval of my performance and her belief in me was more than I ever realized I needed. Even with our differences for the first time I felt a true connection with my sibling. We were true sisters and without words spoken, we realized we were proud to be!

Today my sister is in Heaven. I will always cherish that memory of her. I will never forget not only her belief in me, but also the connection of our hearts that day which can never be replaced. That day, she became my number one fan!

God also wants to be our number one fan. Cheering us on, He wants to be there to watch us perform. He wants to share in the greatest moments of our lives and through them show us just how much He loves us. What is it today He wants to prove rewarding in your life? Take time to ask your Father. Take time today to hear Him tell you where He wants to carry you from here.

*"The Lord delights in those who fear Him,*
*who put their hope in His unfailing love."*
*Psalm 147:11 (NIV)*

# SLAP DAB INTO THE BAIT

The one outdoor activity I love, love, love, to do is fish! When my husband and I first began dating, his brother and wife loved the sport as much as me. Often on the weekends, I'd spend the night with them just so we could wake up at four o'clock a.m. to hit the lake. We always packed the car the night prior with fishing poles, lawn chairs, and tackle boxes. Then in the morning we only required our cups and a thermos of coffee. With the car loaded and much anticipation, we drove to Lake Allatoona for a hopeful day of catching.

Sitting on the lake bank in the silence in the morning was breathtaking. It felt so good just to relax and admire all of God's creation. I watched and anxiously awaited a tug on my bobber. Once the nibbling began, it was only a few more moments until the bait was inhaled, along with the hook. The bobber was under water and my catch frantically swimming for his life. Gladly, I reeled in that long awaited prize!

How often have we all, too, lived like that of a fish? Swimming along, minding our own business and then it seems like out of nowhere, we run slap dab right into the bait. At first it's a curious nibble. Then we seemingly want way more. The bait tastes so good that our minds tell us it's mandatory we have what we now crave. Allowing ourselves to partake in that savory flavor, before we know it, we are hooked! Not only are our minds deranged, but also our bodies are completely overtaken in the addictive behavior. Panic stricken, we run for our lives knowing that the further we run, the deeper the hook penetrates.

God's Word specifically warns us to run for our lives before we nibble on the bait. He directs us to pass it by or swim away long before the nibbling becomes deadly. Fortunately for us, unlike the fish, God is faithful to reel us in. On the shore He guides us home. He gently dislodges the hook and then places us back in the water of life. With a new start, He sets us free from the dark waters. He restores us from the things that have skillfully hooked us tight. God, the Father, patiently stands and waits until He hears our cries. And just like a Father, He lovingly welcomes us back.

Where are you today in the sea of life? Are you swimming safely or being enticed by the bait of everyday destruction? Come home dear one, to the loving Father today. Come back, friend. Your Father in Heaven wants to restore and make you whole. If you will only believe, unhooked, He will guide your way for eternity.

*"I will rescue you from your own people and from the Gentiles.*
*I am sending you to them to open their eyes and turn them*
*from darkness to light, and from the power of satan to God,*
*so that they may receive forgiveness of sins and a place*
*among those who are sanctified by faith in me."*
*Acts 26: 17-18 (NIV)*

# WE DO

*L*iving in a beautiful two-story home on a hill, my parents used it as a wedding chapel; A chapel for my finance and me. The weather had been horrible every weekend since the New Year except this one. It was St. Patrick's Day, March 17, 1979. The sun was shinning, the flowers were blooming, and the weather was warm. God provided the perfect day for this unforgettable event.

That Saturday was a very eventful day including breakfast with the family, decorating the cakes, setting up chairs, arranging the flowers and candles, and getting dressed. I was so very excited!

Respectful of tradition, my finance arrived and stayed in my parent's camper in the backyard until it was time to stand before the crowd. I cheated though; looking out my parent's window I caught a glimpse of my husband to be. It wasn't on purpose. It just happened! Regardless, we both anxiously waited for four o'clock p.m.

My best friend was my Maid-of-Honor and my sister a bridesmaid. My finance's oldest brother was his Best Man and other brother his groomsman. It was a family affair. The only ones who were missing were my finance's parents. They were in Egypt working with his father's job. Because of their absence, they sent us two gold goblets with our names inscribed in English and Hebrew. We used them at our reception.

The staircase in my parent's home began at the foyer so when my daddy and I came down, the crowd stood, turned around and watched as we walked down the aisle. I could see my finance's face and was happier that day than no other in my entire life. I did not realize that much joy even existed! I felt like a princess, a queen and a bride like no other. God had answered my prayers and delivered the man of my dreams!

Hosting 150 guests, the ceremony was beautiful. Friends from my childhood, school, and college attended. Family members came from miles away. My childhood friend played the violin and one of my finance's friends sang a wedding song. My pastor married us. Everything I dreamed of came true. It was a wonderful day to begin our future together.

Spending our honeymoon in Gatlinburg, Tennessee and Cherokee, North Carolina, we will always cherish this time in our lives. We still are reminded of that glorious trip every Christmas when we hang the first ornament we bought that weekend. These memories and moments of long ago will be dear in our hearts forever! The most important day in the history of our lives!

What about you? Has God given you a moment you will cherish forever? Has He delivered a promise or are you still waiting? Take time today to thank Him for His love for you. Take time today to realize that He purposes to lavish you with His love giving you the very best He's got.

*"God will lavish you with good things; children from your womb,*
*offspring from your animals, and crops from your land, that land that*
*God promised your ancestors that He would give you"*
*Deuteronomy 28:11 (The Message)*

# THE
# REST OF THE
# STORIES

# MY LITTLE MIRACLE

To be a mother was something I had always dreamed of even as far back as my pre-teen years. I, like most young girls, anxiously waited for that day of motherhood. I can vividly remember loving to play house as a little girl. My sister and I would pretend to be neighbors. We each had our own pretend baby and our own Cinderella prince. Reenacting the role my mother so wonderfully performed, was natural for me. I dreamed of the day that I also could be the perfect wife and mother like her!

Just as I had dreamed, God sent me the most amazing husband! We were married on March 17, 1979 and thrilled about the life ahead of us! Soon after we were married, I went for my first yearly medical exam. Not expecting anything out of the ordinary to be wrong, I was in complete shock when my doctor informed me that my womb was slanted. Because of this, she was afraid getting pregnant would not be an easy task. How in the world could this possibly be? How could I accept this as truth when I had spent my entire life dreaming of the day I would have my own precious baby! I can still remember the heartfelt pain coupled with the crippling fear of not being able to conceive a precious child. . . a baby in my own womb. Sharing the news with my husband, all we could do was believe that God had different plans. We believed that God could repair the very thing within me that could cause such problems.

I laid my agony before God in prayer, as I knew He had planted those dreams within me. I knew that I alone could not have created that deep desire within myself. Knowing that God had a purpose and plan for my life, I eagerly waited in prayerful anticipation of His healing hand.

It was the very next month that I became pregnant. In amazement and excitement, I knew it was God who straightened my womb. Miracles do occur in our lifetime. God performed one on me! My miracle is my precious firstborn son and the four other little lives I conceived!

Has God shown Himself in your life lately? Has He been faithful to perform a miracle for you? Thank Him today for never changing. Thank Him continually for the love He has for you!

*"Jesus Christ is the same yesterday and today and forever."*
*Hebrews 13:8 (NIV)*

# WHAT TO WEAR?

$\mathcal{I}$ was expecting my first child and I can tell you I was big, and not to mention, very miserable! It was December and very cold outside. My husband and I were invited to a Sunday evening church service to attend a Christmas program that some of the local church members were performing for the community. During this time in our lives, we did not attend church on a regular basis. We had not found a place of worship we were comfortable joining. Consequently, we just didn't go!

Agreeing to visit the church and to get out for a while, I put on some warm maternity pants and a dressy sweater. Because I was so miserable at this point in my pregnancy, I was just ready to get there and find a place to sit down! About to head out the door, my mother-in-law turned and noticed my attire. Kindly, she warned me that my pants would be frowned upon. A little startled at her statement, I questioned her. *"The church does not allow women to wear pants,"* she said. I'm not sure if I was more disappointed or just plain discouraged. I just started crying and changed my clothes. Having to redress with panty hose, a big frumpy dress and heels, I unwillingly went to church that evening with freezing legs!

I can tell you this situation has bothered me for many years. I do understand the respect issue in the House of God but what about the heart? Does God really look at our outward appearance? I have always believed that God doesn't care what we look like when we worship Him. He just wants us to worship! He wants His children to freely come into His presence and lavish in His love. Sitting, standing, laying, weeping, shouting, singing, praying, God doesn't care. He knows our heart's condition. All He wants is us!

Times have changed. Rules have changed. Even dress codes aren't the same as they were thirty plus years ago. One thing that has not changed is God. He still loves us, knows us, wants us and adores us. His desire is for His people to come into His presence. With a pure heart in awe of who He is and what He has done for us, our hearts are all that matters. It's in our willingness to go before Him that He invites us to draw near.

What about you? When was the last time you sat before your King? When was the last time you gave your all for the all He gave for you? Take time today to stand before His throne. Take time to lavish in His love and His awesome unmatchable presence.

*"Let us draw near to God with a sincere heart and with the full assurance that*
*faith brings, having our hearts sprinkled to cleanse us from a guilty conscience*
*and having our bodies washed with pure water. Let us hold unswervingly*
*to the hope we profess, for He who promised is faithful"*
*Hebrews 10:22-23 (NIV)*

# INCREDIBLE SIZE

It was a Tuesday morning when I stood with the front door open and looked back one more time. In that very moment I knew my husband's life and mine would never be the same. Checking into Douglas General Hospital, in Douglasville, GA, I was scheduled to be induced to deliver our first child. Unlike this day in time, I had not been told my baby's sex. We didn't want to know. To us, half of the surprise was finding out the sex when the baby was delivered!

I was a young mother of 23 and somewhat anxious. At this point, my body had been stretched to the "max." I could not get up alone from a sitting position. I could barely even walk. Being short waisted didn't help any either! There was just no more room for this child to grow. My husband was faithful to walk me, pull me up, and support me throughout the entire pregnancy. This day was no exception. He never left my side. He was an incredible husband!!!

In the days of much recommended 'natural births,' I chose a midwife and we successfully graduated from Lamaze classes. Ready to use our newfound skills, the day was off to an exciting start. The medication that was used to begin the labor was also one that increases the intensity and amount of contractions. It was intense alright! With such a large baby, I labored for thirteen hours with no dilation. My blood pressure continued to rise so the doctors agreed a C-Section was the safest procedure for both my baby and me.

Scared and unnerved, I was rolled away to surgery. Still having contractions and lying on my back was a horrible feeling. It was the most excruciating pain I had ever endured. Worried about the medication getting to my baby, they assured me very little would. Before I knew it, I was out. I counted backwards from 100 and I think I remember only 99. Successfully, however, they did wake me up moments later announcing the arrival of my precious baby boy. He was so big, the doctors were betting on how much he actually weighed. Again, I was out and my husband joined the nursery team with our son. He was beautiful and completely healthy! He weighted an unbelievable 9 pounds, 12 ounces, and was 22 1/2 inches long. He literally looked like a three month old next to the other babies in the nursery!

There is no other incredible feeling on earth than the moment your very own child is born. Our son was a miracle to us. We were so very proud and thankful that God entrusted this new life in our care. Life has truly never been the same!

What about you? Has God blessed you with the miracle of a child? Has He entrusted you with the responsibility of raising one of His own? If so, know today that He has chosen you for the most incredible position on earth. Take time today to cry out for the wisdom it takes to raise the child He gave you to be just like his/her Heavenly Father.

*"Start children off on the way they should go, and
even when they are old they will not turn from it.*
*Proverbs 22:6 (NIV)*

# IN DESPERATION

*I*t was my baby boy's first birthday. I had to work but throughout the day I was constantly reminded of a year ago when I gave birth! Although I had not really wanted to return to work, I had too. Fortunately, I found a wonderful woman to babysit my son. She was from my mother-in-law's church and had three children of her own. I felt so much better about him staying there instead of a somewhere where I knew no one!

As usual, I was busy at my job taking care of the day's duties when my phone rang. It was my babysitter on the other line. It took me a minute to recognize her voice because she was screaming so frantically. I immediately thought something must be wrong with my baby. Instead I heard her shout, *"It's my husband! He just shot himself! Get here quick!"* Rushing to the car, one of my co-workers and I sped to her house. The entire way I was beside myself. Not knowing if my son was OK and then not sure of what I'd find when we arrived was more than nerve racking! Finally reaching her house, I jumped out of the car and ran to the door.

My son was safe in the playpen when I ran inside but the rest was a horrible scene. Her husband had come home from work early and seemed a little upset. He went into the bedroom, closed the door and then proceeded to lock himself in the bathroom. As she and the children played in the living room, she heard a gunshot from the back of the house. Running into the bedroom, she found their bathroom door locked. She had no idea what she would find on the other side. Panicked, she dialed 911.

The paramedics were on the bedroom floor trying to revive him when I arrived. He had shot himself in the chest and was not breathing. He was already gone. Her husband had successfully taken his own life.

Thankfully, my son does not remember that day. I will never forget it, however. In a moment's time, this man went from life to death. He went from possessing breath to having none. The story of his life ended there. The story of his family's future changed forever!

God has promised to be a comforter in our time of need. He knows our desperate moments. He hears our desperate cries. When we need Him and we have no energy to even cry, He is there as well. He was there that day for my friend. She was desperate and God showed up. Although her husband wasn't there for her anymore, God was. He never left.

What about you? Has there been a time in your life you were desperate for God? Have you experienced a moment where you could not even cry out? Fear not, my friend. God is always there. He will never leave us even in our weakest moments. He is the only one who can make us strong in our weaknesses. Cry out to Him today knowing that you belong to the Savior; knowing you are His indeed!

*"Desperate, I throw myself on you: you are my God!"*
*Psalm 31:14 (The Message)*

# HIS SWEET WORDS

*W*hen my husband and I got together, we were blessed with two sets of wonderful parents. Dating for a year and a half we were fortunate to have them all in our lives. Just prior to our wedding day, however, my father-in-law accepted an overseas job with his company that required him and his wife to move to Dubai. Sadly, they were not present for our big wedding day. One year and six months after returning home, my father-in-law accepted another job out of the country. Unfortunately, we were only two weeks away from welcoming our first-born son. My husband's father missed that incredible event in our lives too. Finally when I was pregnant a second time with our first baby girl, my husband's dad died suddenly of a heart attack and went to be with the Lord! My father-in-law missed three of the most exciting events my husband and I experienced.

Tucked away in my son's baby book is a letter I often read. The sweet words of a man who would never be a part of the most eventful times in his son's life. Saddened by his absence, we held onto his words of adoration from that letter. Words that captured our hearts as we read how proud he was of us. Still treasuring that letter today, we are always reminded of the wonderful man he was to both of us!

God, as His only source, escorted this man of obedience to a better place. His walk, his talk, and his testimony remained in the lives of those who best knew him. As I gaze upon that note he wrote I somehow know that God left a piece of him with us forever. If his presence were here, I am convinced he would have never spoken those words. Instead of dictated echoes for only our minds to hear his feelings were recorded on paper left for generations to come.

Has God recorded the sweet words of a loved one for you? How is it your Father has seen you through even when you could not share those times with the ones you loved so dear? Ask Him today to recall the words of old for you. Ask Him today to help you step back in time to remember the life of someone who has gone before.

*"The Lord gave and the Lord has taken away;*
*may the name of the Lord be praised."*
*Job 1:21b (NIV)*

# WHERE DID HE GO?

*M*y children were just like yours I'm sure. Normal kids. They had their days when they'd fight. They were loud at times. They also had their own individual expressions and ideas about things.

One afternoon after church, my husband and I took the two oldest children, who were one and six, to a nearby Shoney's restaurant. As usual, the place was packed. The waitress finally escorted us to a table and we proceeded to talk about what we would all like to have for lunch. Because the children normally wasted food, as parents, we always dictated their order from the menu. Realizing they had to share, the complaining began. The kid's disappointment was expressed with loud voices and disruption that nearly sent my husband into orbit. Now, my husband wasn't very accustom to outings in public with our more than typical offspring. In fact, at home he just never really paid much attention. Arriving home near bedtime and working during the daytime didn't allow him much time to even see the children they were. Dads are usually clueless due to the stresses of their job requirements. As moms, however, we just learn to ignore, correct as needed and then simply move forward.

That Sunday afternoon lunch time outing was filled with loud talking, the kids disagreeing, and just the normalness of life; at least to me. For my husband, it was not such a glorious day. Where I just allowed the little things to roll off my back, he, on the other hand, went into a tailspin. Before I knew it, he requested the ticket and slipped away from our family's table. Watching and waiting for his return, I look out the restaurant window to find him relaxing and family-less waiting in the car.

God has made us all uniquely. He "knitted us together" in our own distinctive way. In fact, He knew what He was doing. In doing what He does best, create, He isn't surprised at our differences. It's because of that He intentionally places us together with those that most often are complete opposites. He knows us individually and stitches us together anyway. His plan in that is to make us better and to make us more like Him in His very image. And no matter, unlike how we may react and do, He promises to never leave us, even if we hang with the task or silently slip away from it all.

What is it today you see differently than another? How is it that God has made you different? Take time today to realize that the salt and pepper people in life are ideal to complete the final touch. Two different but equally needed spices to complete a very satisfying meal.

*"For you created my inmost being; you knit me together in my mother's womb.*
*I praise you because I am fearfully and wonderfully made;*
*your works are wonderful. I know that full well."*
*Psalm 139:13-14 (NIV)*

# THE TRIP OF A LIFETIME

When my husband and I prepared to celebrate our tenth anniversary, we knew we wanted to take a trip to somewhere very special. We also knew we wanted to leave the state of Georgia where we lived, but weren't sure exactly where we should go.

Working for a retail company, my husband won two airline tickets that could be used within the United States. That was a blessing and our way of getting to our dream destination. Then, even more of a miracle, my friend who was also from Georgia, contacted me asking if I would come to her wedding to be her Maid of Honor. The greatest part was she lived in Hawaii where she was stationed with her husband serving in the United States Navy! Not only having airline tickets and then a place to stay, our trip was planned!

With great anticipation, my husband and I made the journey. Arriving in Hawaii, it was as beautiful as we had always heard. Staying on Waikiki Beach in Honolulu was next to heaven! The beach was breathe taking, the weather was absolutely wonderful, and the scenery was more than words could describe! It was a dream come true!

Arriving at the courthouse, we met my dear friend for her wedding. It was a beautiful ceremony and she was a gorgeous bride. I was so pleased to be able to be there with her on her special day! Because of her travels with the Navy, we had spent the past two years only seeing one another at Christmas. It was wonderful spending the week with her and her new husband!

Our trip was amazing. Not only seeing my friend, but the island itself. While we were there, we took advantage of our time and tried to see as much as possible. We attended a Luau, flew to the island of Maui for an overnight stay and saw the U.S.S. Arizona at Pearl Harbor. Coupled with history and beauty, we will never forget our trip. It was most definitely a second honeymoon to remember. A trip of a lifetime!

Sometimes we dream of things God smiles about. In His goodness, He allows our plans to succeed. Working out the details, He sees to it that our dreams come true. Giving Him the glory, I know that not only did He provide a way for me to see my dear friend and support her on one of the most memorable days of her life, but also for my husband and me to celebrate our marriage of ten years. He indeed provided for us. He indeed knew the desires of our hearts and made a way for everything to become a reality.

What dream has God given you? What is it you know only God can work out on your behalf? Take time today to go to your Father and present your request. Allow time to share with Him your hearts desires. If you don't know Him today, take time to give your life to Him so that you will be guaranteed a life unimaginable; a life of complete adventure, surrender and anticipation of where He will take you from here!

*"Delight yourself in the Lord and He will give*
*you the desires of your heart."*
*Psalm 37:4 (ESV)*

# THE PERFECT SCARS

*L*ike most people, I have several scars that are permanently tattooed on my body. Over the years, I've acquired these marks and many have a story, but not every one gives an obvious explanation.

As every woman knows, you create scars from wounds of shaving. Yes, I have acquired nicks, cuts, slashes and gouges from this much warranted womanly 'sport.' Fortunately, their sizes aren't too extreme compared to others. I do have one scar that is situated on the right side of my face, very close to my temple. My middle daughter and I were washing my station wagon. I bent over to dry the car door when I raised my head up way too quickly. Completely taken off guard, the side mirror met my face and gashed it wide open. The wound looks just like a half moon. It's only about a half inch wide but it's still very visual. It always causes me to remember that day. Now, when I see a small child walk too close to a vehicle, I unconsciously put my hand on the mirror to guard them from being cut too!

You would naturally think that one would learn from past scars how to avoid them. Not! In fact, as my skin becomes older and more worn, scaring is more achievable. My arms and hands have more burn marks from cooking now than I ever received when I raised my children. I can't figure out if it's because I just didn't scar as much then or what. Even so, they are everywhere!

Scars do mark us. They provide evidence of what transpired when we received them. Some good ones. Some bad ones. Some because of pain. Some because of loss. Some because of gain. Most scars are totally unexpected ones but some, we certainly make on purpose! Nevertheless, they mark more than our skin. They mark our memories!

God, too, understands scars. He understands the memories and moments that come with each mark. There were some scars He even purposed! On a cross at Calvary, His own Son was nailed to a tree. He suffered and died for you and me. As evidence, His hands, His feet, and His side were pierced. His heart was engaged as well. His scars were to benefit the human race. When He hung on that tree, He bore all the sins mankind would ever face. Yesterday, today and forever!

What about you? Do you know the One who experienced the greatest scars of all? Take time today to be certain you know the Son of God who bore His scars for you. Know without a doubt that your scars are covered with the blood of the Lamb!

*"Just as there were many who were appalled at Him–His*
*appearance was so disfigured beyond that of any human*
*being and His form marred beyond human likeness—"*
*Isaiah 52:14 (NIV)*

# WHO DONE IT?

My mother-in-law planned every summer not only to work at her church's annual Vacation Bible School, but to have all of her grandchildren attend as well. There were a total of six grandkids. She housed them all for a week until the closing night's festivities on Sunday evening. By the end of the week, however, she was spent. Her nerves were shot, the kids were wild, and she was more than ready to get back to her quiet single life!

One particular afternoon, after they had returned from a fun filled morning, she decided to lie down and rest. She demanded the kids do the same. They were all sent to the living room to find a resting place, watch television, and just chill. Right! As she was sleeping, it got a little wild to say the least. Wrestling around, as normal boys do, my son and his cousin got a little too close to her handmade ceramic lamp, a matching set of which she was so proud. In the course of their scuffling, the lamp went crashing to the floor. The lamp broke completely in half. Overcome with fear the boys hurriedly placed the lamp back together where it had cracked and carefully sat it back in its place. Without hesitation, they all sat quietly until their grandmother came in a few hours later to watch TV with them.

As their grandmother reached over to turn on her prize lamp, it instantly toppled over and broke into many more pieces. Furious, she knew one of the guilty parties was positioned in a seat in that very living room. Funny thing is that even after the passing of my mother-in-law, none of those children have ever admitted their guilt. Too afraid to tell on the other, I'm pretty sure that well-kept secret will surely die with them!

How often in our own lives have we been fooling around, not really meaning to end up in a broken situation? Things start out to be just fun, but in the end the fun turns out disastrous. In the midst of the disaster, we run scared and swear we will never again go back to that moment in time. Stored within, still lies the secret of the who, what, when and where of our unspeakable situation.

What is it today you need to go back and revisit? What is it you need God to help you confront? Ask Him today to be your guide. Ask Him to gently repair the broken pieces of the mistakes you have chosen to forget. Allow Him to clean up your mess so that you can breathe without fear and move forward with the comfort of a clear and eased conscience.

*"My conscience is clear, but that does not make me*
*innocent. It is the Lord who judges me."*
*1 Corinthians 4:4 (NIV)*

# TO BE THE FATHER

*A*fter having two cesarean section births of my own, I had never witnessed a natural birth. My best friend's wife was about to deliver their first baby and asked me to be in the delivery room. I was so excited! The daddy, my best friend, was a weakling. He got weak to his knees every time the thought of the delivery was mentioned. In fact, he was elated to have me stand in as the "father."

On September 1, 1988, my friend's labor began. At first, she labored at home and then when she finally went to the hospital, I was called. Arriving at labor and delivery, I found her almost ready to have their baby. Because I was a voice major, I always told her I wanted to be the first to sing to her newborn. This was long before I knew I would have the position of "father" as well. Preparing to meet this baby, I stood beside her, along with her sister, and coached her the best I knew how. She pushed and pushed and finally we saw the head. Before we could believe it, a precious baby boy made his way into the world! It was 1:01 p.m. With tears of joy, we all clapped and cried as he cried! I'm still not sure who was the loudest!

Once he was cleaned up, the nurse handed me their baby. Standing in the midst of that nursery room, I began singing "Amazing Grace." It was such a sobering moment. Looking at this new life that God had purposed, planned and anointed, I was filled with emotion. His little face, with sparkling eyes, stared at mine while he intensely but quietly listened as I sang. To this day, I will never forget that priceless moment. God was most definitely there!

Giving him back to his mommy, it was time to announce his birth to his real daddy. Walking down the hall, I could hardly hold back the tears. Opening up the double doors to the waiting room, I saw his face. Time stood still for a moment. "*It's a precious baby boy*," I screamed! Hugging and crying, we both made our way back to the delivery room for him to see his son. What a glorious day it was, a day I'll never forget!

God has purposed every life He creates. He knows us each one long before we are ever in our mother's womb. He has a perfect plan for every life. The choice is ours, however, to either follow His lead and walk out that plan or do it all on our own.

Take time today to evaluate whether you are walking the path God has set out before you or are you simply wondering around. If you are following His lead, thank Him for His direction. If not, take time to recognize your need for His guidance in your life today! He will gladly show you how.

*"Before I formed you in the womb I knew you, before you were born*
*I set you apart; I appointed you as a prophet to the nations."*
*Jeremiah 1:5 (NIV)*

# OUR BABY HANNAH

One evening in November 1990, as I was reading my Bible, God clearly spoke to me. Out of nowhere He said, *"For your obedience to submit to your husband and your support to move from place to place and believe in him, I am going to give you a baby girl. Her name will be Hannah!"* I was speechless! I was thrilled! I was in shock but I knew I couldn't tell a soul. With my husband in another state, I also knew this would certainly be tricky! As quickly as God spoke these words, however, He erased them from my memory. I literally forgot in an instant.

Unable to sell our home by March of 1991, I was ready to get back to normal of sorts. My husband and I decided to go ahead and move us across country and believe God that our Arizona home would soon have a buyer. Fortunately, we were able to move in with my mother-in-law. My former employer was eager to rehire me as well. Thankfully, my seniority and insurance would be effective the day I started!

Like planned, we moved, set up new residency back in Georgia and I began work on April 1. Two months after staring work, I went to lunch with a friend. I had not felt well for the past week but continued to work. Over our meal my friend looked me dead in the eyes and said, "I think you're pregnant!' Startled and shocked, I argued with her. Brushing off her statement, we returned to work.

Later in the week I was reminded of her words. Not feeling any better I decided to stop by the drugstore on the way home and invest in a pregnancy test. By then, I knew if I wasn't pregnant, I was probably dying of a dreaded disease! Anticipating the results and daring not to tell anyone, I took the test. To my surprise, the test was positive! Suddenly, the words God spoke to me flowed back to my memory. *"For your obedience, I will give you a baby girl. You will name her Hannah."*

God knows all about the greatest plans for our lives. Thinking we have all things worked out, He knows what we need the most. He will make a way where there seems to be no way. He will provide every need and He is faithful to hear and meet the desires of our hearts even when we think they will never be. I am proof of that! Today, we are grateful for our baby girl, Hannah!

What is it today that you desire deep down? What has God spoken to you that maybe you have forgotten? Ask Him today to stir up your deep longings within so that you may see His glorious plan take action! He has buried desires deep within. Allow Him today to begin the process of bringing forth your miracle!

> *"In her deep anguish Hannah prayed to the Lord, weeping bitterly. And she made a vow, saying, "Lord Almighty, if you will only look on your servant's misery and remember me, and not forget your servant but give her a son, then I will give him to the Lord for all the days of his life, and no razor will ever be used on his head." As she kept on praying to the LORD, Eli observed her mouth."*
> *1 Samuel 1: 10-11 (NIV)*

# PANIC MODE

*W*hen I answered the phone, all I could hear was the panic stricken voice of my mother-in-law on the other line. She was frantic and wanted me home immediately! The woods behind the house were suddenly on fire.

My son and his cousin were staying with their grandmother for the day. She was on one side of the property hanging clothes on the clothesline while the boys were on the opposite end behind the shed. One of them had taken a pack of matches from the house. They decided it would be fun to start a small fire behind the shed. Even though they had only planned for a little fire, the wind and underbrush dictated another story. Wind blowing and dry brush made way for an excellent wave of moving flames. Stomping with all of their might, the boys worked frantically trying to get control of the now consuming fire. My son's cousin quickly ran to get the water hose but it wasn't long enough to stretch to the open flames. With no other choice, screaming like little girls, the boys ran to get their grandmother. She was their only rescue. Unfortunately, by this time the fire was completely out of control. Overall, it burned five acres of her land.

When I finally arrived home, it looked like a war zone. There were five fire trucks in her driveway. Firefighters were everywhere. Out of the corner of my eye, I caught a glimpse of the two boys. The fire chief was having a stern conversation with both of the culprits! Matches were soon ban from their reach and a fire safety course was on their agenda!

Just like the boys, there are times our curiosity leads us to do what we know we shouldn't. We allow the enticement of the wrong we know to capture us in a sticky web of deceit. Before we know it, we are panic stricken doing our best to clean up the mess. The bad part is we usually can't do it on our own. We need the help of an expert. One who is experienced in cleaning up our messes!

Have you found yourself in a sticky web of deceit recently? Are you perhaps working franticly trying to clean up the mess you've made? Take time today to allow God to take hold of your situation. Allow Him to make a miracle out of your mess!

*"Do not merely listen to the word, and so deceive yourselves. Do what it says."*
*James 1:22 (NIV)*

# UNEXPECTED EXPECTING

*I* was 39 and by this time, it seemed life was quickly passing by. Our oldest son was 16 and preparing to drive. Our middle child was in middle school and my baby was starting kindergarten. For the first time since childbearing years, I was at home without an infant. Three years prior, my husband had a vasectomy. We both agreed our three offspring were all we needed to complete our family tree.

One day, while the children were in school and my husband out of town, I made the normal trip to run some errands. For days I hadn't felt well and that day was no exception. Even though I knew better, I couldn't shake the fact that my symptoms were the same as with my three former pregnancies. Knowing a vasectomy prevents that possibility I still couldn't shake that feeling. Not telling a soul, I made my way into a local drug store and bought a pregnancy test. Returning home, I took the test. Anxiously awaiting the results, I almost vomited. As I had unexplainably expected, I WAS PREGNANT. At this point, I was also frantic! I didn't know how this could have possibly happened.

Knowing my next step was to try to explain this all to my husband, I sent a "911" message to his pager. Once he called, I revealed our unexpected dilemma. Although being as shocked as I, he quickly consoled and assured me all would be ok. Unfortunately it was not. Two weeks later, my doctor's appointment concluded there was no heartbeat. Our fourth child was no longer. Completely crushed and overwhelmingly heartbroken, we both grieved the loss of our precious child.

Sometimes life throws a curve ball. Most of the time, it's when you least expect it. Although we had made the adjustments, my husband's surgery had reversed itself. Thinking another pregnancy could never happen we were both proved wrong. Life will prove you wrong many times. It will also bring about the unexpected. No matter, there is hope. No matter, there is a Savior who is there to walk you through any trial. Even when you least expect it, things can turn completely around. When you think you have it all together, things can fall apart. The good news is God is there is help you. He is there to calm your sea of unbelief. He is there to restore your broken spirit. Even when you find no answers, He will always lead you through. He will always offer you hope in the tragedies of your days. Without Him, I know I'd be a total mess!

What about you? Are there unexplainable occurrences you've had to endure? Are there moments you were knocked off your feet? Allow the healer of life to pick you up. Allow Him to restore your brokenness today!

*"In all this you greatly rejoice, though now for a little while you*
*may have had to suffer grief in all kinds of trials."*
*1 Peter 1:6 (NIV)*

# HER PREDICTED FALL

One summer day, my son, middle daughter and baby girl made a trip to a local hardware store. With my husband out of town, I had to take all three children with me to shop. Loving to admire the many selections of plants and patio furniture, I usually would go alone so I could take my time and browse. This trip I knew I'd have to get in, find what I was shopping for and get out. Not one of my children loved shopping near as much as I did!

My baby daughter was two and big enough to sit in the back of the buggy. She was always very good to mind me. I had never had a problem with her standing in the buggy so I continued to let her sit there. The other two children were also obedient to stay right beside me when we shopped.

Needing to step away from the cart to find an item I was looking for, I ask my then thirteen-year-old son to keep an eye on his little sister. I told him to stand at the back of the buggy where his sister was sitting to ensure she wouldn't for some reason decide to stand. I knew a fall onto a concrete slab would not be a very pretty picture! Agreeing to watch her, I stepped away to the other aisle. No sooner did I turn the corner I heard a scream. Running with all of my might, as I rounded the corner I saw my little girl lying on the concrete. Her head was red and purple from the slam on to the floor. I scooped her up in my arms and briskly walked right out of the store. I was so angry with my son for not doing what I ask him to do. Why couldn't I have trusted him for one second? Why couldn't he just have been obedient to do what I asked him to do? I told him what would happen if he didn't do what I ask of him and obviously he wasn't paying attention. Fortunately, my daughter had no permanent damage or scar. She just suffered from the pain of that hard floor banging her head and the fear she felt as she fell. Understandingly, she hates the thought of going back to that establishment. It brings to mind her fall every time she thinks of that place!

God understood my frustration and anger that day. He, too, knows what it's like to warn His children of danger and He knows the pain of seeing His loved ones suffer because they refuse to listen and obey! We are those children and you and I are guilty as charged.

Fortunately, He forgives, heals our bruises and restores us back to normal. He offers us the ability to repent, turn and obey His Word. Knowing that His Word is compiled with instruction that never fails, He tells us it's in our best interest to follow. Even though we can't see what's up ahead, He can. He knows. Why in the world wouldn't we want to take heed to the one who sees and knows all long before we do? Ask yourself that very question today.

*"Your obedience will give you a long life on the soil that*
*God promised to give your ancestors and their children,*
*a land flowing with milk and honey."*
*Deuteronomy 11:9 (The Message)*

# FORWARDING HIS WORDS

*B*efore my sister passed away, my mom's best friend suddenly died of a heart attack. No warnings. Just death. It was very hard for her husband and her children. My sister was also battling her own death call with cancer. Knowing her day was soon to come, she still attended our family friend's funeral.

Two weeks later, sure enough, my only sister lay in wait for her last breath. That morning, the husband of our friend who had just passed away happened to be in the neighborhood. Knowing my sister wasn't doing well, he stopped by to check on her. Unknowing of her condition that day, immediately he knew that our family was quietly waiting for her exit. Running home to get something, he told us he'd soon be back.

The evening before, my sister slipped into a comatose state. Knowing that hearing is the last sense to go, I continually told her it was ok for her to die. I knew it was better for her to go and be with her Savior. I assured her we would take care of her children. She still hung on. For hours she hung on.

Early afternoon, our friend's husband returned. He brought with him his wife's favorite cross. Sitting on my sister's beside, he talked for a while. He asked my sister to tell his wife the things he never got to say. He asked her to let her know how much he loved her and missed her. He laid the cross by my sister's pillow and left her room. Within a few minutes, my sister showed signs of leaving this earth. Her breathing became more labored and then she took her last breath. She stepped from the pain of this earth to the wellness of heaven.

Little did I know that even in her death, God had a plan. Although our friend's wife died suddenly, God made a way for her husband to say his last goodbyes. God allowed a grieving husband to experience peace even in the midst of extreme tragedy. Although I could not understand why my sister would not go ahead and die, God had something more for her to do. Little did I know that God was using my sibling while in her last breaths to deliver a much-needed message that no one else could deliver. Isn't that just so God?

What about your life? Has He something He needs for you to do? Is He preparing to use you even in the midst of tragedy? Has He chosen you to deliver a message of hope? Take time today to ask Him what it is He'd have you do. Ask Him today to lead the way.

*"And He is not served by human hands, as if He needed anything. Rather He*
*Himself gives everyone life and breath and everything else."*
*Acts 17:25 (NIV)*

# DEATH'S STING

Although the sting of death is one of the most unpredicted, heart changing events in life, one day, we will each be faced with it's grip. My first taste was as a little girl of eleven years. Three of my grandparents took that final step from life on earth to eternity. An unpleasant fear engulfed me for years to come after those experiences!

When my Dad's mother died in March of 1970, I clearly remember sitting next to my cousins during her funeral. To keep from being tagged a crybaby, I repetitively pinched myself to bring my emotions under control. In somewhat of a time when most children cried because of a simple knee scrape or the sting of a fresh picked hickory switch, I was experiencing much deeper pain.

The day of my grandmother's funeral was bad enough, but as our family and friends began to disperse from the graveside, I can still today visualize my sweet Daddy whaling with sorrow as He realized he would have to let go of his precious mother. Hanging onto the bronze casket, draped with a spray of flowers, Dad was completely out of control crying, "*Mama! Mama!*"

Only a month later, April escorted my Mom's dad to be with the Lord. As the family again gathered at the funeral home, the moment came when the nice men dressed in suits, escorted us into this room with my granddaddy. It was time to say our last good-byes. As the gentlemen began to move towards the casket to close his body within, my mother gave way to a flood of disbelief. Crying out with that same sound, "Daddy, Daddy," she fell onto his chest with a clinging grip. Patiently, they waited as she also said her last good-bye.

As the clock chimed noon on Wednesday, January 29, 1996, my sister lay in that same state, as the older woman in me prepared to let her go. Nearly climbing the very walls that surrounded me, I again heard my daddy scream, "*my baby, my baby.*" Today as my mind races back to that desperately lonely child of yesteryears, all the memories of those horrid sounds flood my mind. Letting go was so very difficult, yet for the first time, I could relate to the giving up that I had seen both of my parents do some 26 years earlier.

God has a way of providing a numbing effect within us until the healing is complete. One day, though, I will be reunited with those I love so much. In that moment, together, we will see Jesus' face!

Who is it that you will meet at the gates in that glorious city? Today I ask that the God of restoration restore your broken heart until it is completely repaired in Heaven.

*"Blessed are those who mourn, for they will be comforted."*
*Matthew 5:4 (NIV)*

76

# Her Resting Place

When my sister passed away, after her tragic death, there were arrangements that had to be made. Unfortunately they were plans that we as a family had never thought of or ever even let enter our minds. Sadly, we were faced with this task when we would have much rather had her in our presence.

The evening of her death, my mother took on the responsibility of choosing the perfect wig that would adequately display her beauty. Just a few days before the chemo had caused clumps of her gorgeous long blond hair to fall out. With my sister's direction my mom shaved my sister's head in preparation for her coming days. The wig chosen completely transformed her looks back to the sister I had known.

Besides choosing the casket, vault, spray of flowers, making service and funeral arrangements there was the ordeal of escorting her body after the funeral from one county to another. Several years prior, my sister had worked in dispatch for a local county police department. She had made several close friends while on the job. Those friendships were still in place. County regulations would not allow any county to cross over into another county's jurisdiction. That day, however, counties came together for one cause. Three different counties escorted my sister's body. Those three forces came together for our family to show respect for a fellow sister of the department. Watching the officers stop in one county and then allow the next county to resume the escort was breathtaking. The memory of my sister was exhorted before our very eyes. I know she would have been most gracious at their honoring of her life on earth. For each of us, it was the perfect ending for the most difficult day to date in the history of our family!

No matter what difficulty we face, God is always there to see us through. His mercy and His grace are new every morning. When we cry out to Him for wisdom, strength, courage or grace, He is faithful to deliver. In these times it is God that promises to be there to walk with us through every single situation we face. When our strength has been removed or our peace suddenly sucked from our being, God will restore us and revive us into His image.

What about you? Have you faced death square in the eyes or known someone who has? Take time today to fully realize the love our Father has for us. Take time to know that even in the most difficult hours, just like God was with Jesus in the Garden of Gethsemane prior to His death, He is also with us. Thank Him for loving us enough to never leave or forsake us!

*"For you died, and your life is now hidden with Christ in God."*
*Colossians 3:3 (NIV)*

# FOREVER FRIENDS

Sisters .... Is the proper definition really of the same blood? I am the oldest of a sister and a brother. I am so thankful to God for my only earthly sister. Almost without warning, my sister passed away with cancer in less than three months of her diagnosis. I will treasure the memories of her existence forever.

Once she left this earth to be with her Heavenly Father, God knew I would need new sisters to fill the void I would immediately acquire. Unbeknownst to me, God already had new ones in place. In His goodness, He had already prepared their hearts, laid out the plans, and begun the process of this very important task. My growing older and the experiencing of such severe pain would warrant several new siblings. New sisters that would be the glue that pieced back together my shattered and broken heart.

Faithfully, God did just that. Although while I had many painful days without my blood sister, God was mixing new blood with the new sisters He was sending! In fact, He filled my life with sisters that will remain knitted to my heart for a lifetime! Every close friend that He positioned in my life met a different need. One that could stay with me to assist with my children and remain in our household while my husband traveled. Another who was so much like me. She encouraged the dreams God was bringing to pass and was faithful to help me attain them. And two others God sent to laugh with and make special memories.

God promises to meet our every need. He, too, has riches beyond measure that He graciously wants to give to His precious children. It was in my time of desperate need, God was faithful to provide and plant brand new forever friends. These precious beings would be a beacon in my darkest nights. Oh, how I am blessed. For through the blood of the Lamb, the Spirit of the Living God has graciously performed a miracle in my life. It was through His blood that a transfusion amongst my friends and myself has made us true blood sisters in the name of Christ.

What about you? Has God filled a permanent space in your heart today? Take time to ponder and thank Him for His divine graciousness and love.

*"And my God will meet all your needs according to the*
*riches of His glory in Christ Jesus."*
*Philippians 4:19 (NIV)*

# THE COMFORTER

Trying to recover from a death is very intense. Knowing you have to forfeit ever hearing their voice, feeling their touch or seeing their presence on earth is, to say the least, detrimental! It is life changing!

Two weeks had passed since the death of my sister. Although we didn't live very close anymore, she was still a very important part of my life. Family was everything to me! Life for everyone else had returned to normal while I found myself still very much distressed. Living in Tennessee left me with no other extended family members to lean on during such a tragic time. My husband had returned to his traveling, the kids had gone back to school, and there I was, left, to try and pick up the pieces as I returned to life as I had left it. I really wasn't sure if things could ever be better. Not only my heart, but also my world was crushed!

Each morning after I had put the kids on the school bus, I would quickly retreat back to bed in hopes of sleeping away my day. Hopefully, the Lord would allow me just one more opportunity to dream of her, hear her voice, or feel her presence yet another moment.

One day I went back to bed and while lying there on my side, I cried out to God in total despair. My hurt was so severe that I began to realize the numbness of shock was quickly wearing off. As I prayed to my Father, I could sense His presence begin to flood my bloodstream. As if a blanket of warmth had wrapped itself around me, I suddenly felt a set of arms encamp around my being. This day, as the disciples had once known, I felt the loving arms of God come to my rescue. In that moment of despair the one true Comforter, who knew first hand the sting of death, empathized with me.

What is it today you have experienced only known to the Savior? How has grief seemed unbearable in your own life? Cry out today to the one who is willing to come to your rescue. Let Him know how you need Him to comfort you today.

*"Come to me, all you who are weary and burdened, and I will give you rest. Take my*
*yoke upon you and learn from me, for I am gentle and humble in heart, and you*
*will find rest for your souls. For my yoke is easy and my burden is light."*
*Matthew 11:28-30 (NIV)*

# THE REARRANGEMENT

*M*y two girls stayed with their grandmother while their dad and I were at work. Temporally living with her, the girls became accustomed to making themselves at home.

One afternoon, while my mother-in-law enjoyed a good book, the girls decided to play grocery store. It was my oldest daughter's idea and she easily persuaded her younger sister to play along. Preparing to create the store area, the girls removed all of their grandmother's canned goods from the pantry. Very neatly, they re-stacked the cans on one of the kitchen counters. Knowing a grocery store just isn't complete without a cold and frozen section, the girls decided everything must be displayed. Carefully they removed all the frozen items in her freezer and arranged them in the designated "freezer section." Diligently they removed every item from the refrigerator and neatly placed them in their "cold section." The store was finally stocked and ready for action.

As the girls proudly prepared to open for business, my mother-in-law just happened to walk by the kitchen and glance in at the girls. Almost as quickly as she glanced, she backed up to look again. She was quickly overcome by the sight of her entire food collection displayed before her eyes in her once tidy kitchen. Overcome with shock and disbelief, my mother-in-law's knees buckled and she fell to the floor. Yes, she passed out. The unpredicted upset of her once arranged and organized kitchen had taken a toll on her body so she was out like a light!

Fortunately for her and the girls, she revived pretty quickly. Needless to say, the untidy kitchen was immediately returned to a kitchen less a "grocery store" makeover.

Just like us, often we have clever ideas on how to rearrange what God has placed in perfect order. Removing and rearranging things like we want will change up the very things He has neatly arranged. Fortunately however, God is not surprised at us. Unlike my mother-in-law, He knows our plan making. He knows our creative skills. He loves us enough to step aside and allow us to see that only He can perfectly set up what's best for us.

How about you? Are there areas you continue to still man alone? Are there things you need to release to the Father? Take time today to look around and see from what you need to step back. Take time today to allow God to have the lead. He truly is the only one that can perfectly fill that role.

*"Listen to advice and accept discipline,*
*and in the end you will be counted among the wise."*
*Proverbs 19:20 (NIV)*

# THAT STITCH OF THREAD

*A*fter our home was on the market for six months, it finally sold! Our move from Knoxville, Tennessee to Nashville was going to be a reality! Moving to Nashville would finally allow my children and me to be reunited with my husband after a long year of separation!

One morning, just a few days before we were to close on the sale of the house, we received the unbelievable news that our almost completed Nashville home had been destroyed by fire. I will never forget that afternoon when my husband and I stood in almost total disbelief, amongst the ashes of what was to be our newly purchased home.

Rebuilding would be another three-month process, so the kids and I followed my husband to Georgia while He worked on a company project. Living with my mom and dad, we enjoyed six weeks of much needed family time. My sister was pregnant with her second child and the new arrival would take place just a few days before our departure. The entire event also was the thread that gently stitched the hearts of my childhood best friend and me even tighter after years of separation. Life, sometimes with its changes, has a way of separating even the closest of friends!

Before her expected due date, my second niece was born on August 5, 1994. Fortunately, I was able to witness her arrival. I was also able to videotape her entire grand entrance! The memories of that day will linger in my mind for a lifetime.

In wonder, a few years later, God revealed His purpose of the loss of our newly built home. That strategic heart surgery He performed between my sister and I was the last thread of our unpredictable lives. My sibling, and only sister, was taken from this earth only two years later. Those moments, those remembrances, and those videotaped pictures will be carved in the theatre screen of my mind. God did have a restoration process in place. God did have a greater purpose. In His greatness, He saw what would carry me through even after such an unpredictable tragedy.

How has God seen you through life's changes? Take time today to ponder His mighty handiwork. Take time today to reflect on a major event in your life where God has turned your situation from brokenness to unbelievable restoration.

> *"For I know the plans I have for you, declares the Lord,*
> *plans to prosper you and not to harm you,*
> *plans to give you hope and a future."*
> *Jeremiah 29:11 (NIV)*

# TRAVEL INFORMATION

When my children were two, nine, and fourteen years old, our family moved to Nashville, Tennessee. With my family being Georgia natives, we made quite a few trips back to visit my home. It became a tradition that we stopped at the Georgia Rest Area. That was the halfway point in the trip. The rest area hosted a beautiful building with restrooms, snack machines, and information about the state. My middle daughter especially loved that place. In fact, every time we went, she ran directly to the literature section and grabbed one of every pamphlet that was on display. The rest of the trip, she'd look at every detail of each one like she was studying for a major exam. The problem was, before you knew it, after we arrived back home we would find the remains of all of those information sheets in her room along with all the other thousand she had collected on previous trips.

Pack rat doesn't even describe the likes of my daughter. She was the queen of collecting. Every drawer, every box, every piece of furniture not only hosted trinkets we had given her, but also had become the resting spot for all of her collection of papers. Those papers not only included all of her pamphlets but my unwanted mail I had earlier discarded. That girl had her own idea of what would be considered trash and what was to be stored in her room of clutter!

Today, we still laugh about those thousands of pamphlets. If the truth be known, she probably had enough stored in her room to have restocked the rack in any rest area! She was determined not to throw any of them away. Like her mother always said, "You just never know when you might need something important from one of those pages of valued information!"

How about you? Has God provided you with a collection of valuable information over the years of your life? Has He helped you store up the things you will need to direct your future? Take a look back today. Remind yourself of the things you may need to reexamine. At the same time take the useless stuff and cast it aside before it takes up the space of the vital things so needed in life. Take time today to clean out and tidy up the valued things God has so freely given to guide and provide for you for the remainder of your journey.

*"Do not store up for yourselves treasures on earth, where moth and vermin destroy,*
*and where thieves break in and steal. But store up for yourselves treasures in heaven,*
*where moths and vermin do not destroy, and where thieves do not break in or steal.*
*For where your treasure is, there your heart will be also"*
*Matthew 6:19-20 (NIV)*

# PROUD AS A PEACOCK

My mother-in-law once lived in a small two-bedroom apartment in Tallapoosa, Georgia. The apartments in the complex sat side-by-side and everyone's front yard was nothing but a parking lot. It was a huge parking lot. Every time we visited her, the kids loved to ride their bikes, play football or just run around and play. It really was a great source of outside entertainment.

One particular time we were there, a group of male teenagers packed the parking lot to play a game of football. That day there seemed to be more visitors than normal, therefore creating a great number of onlookers. My eagle-eyed, boy-lovin' niece immediately recognized a perfect opportunity to get the attention of all of those good looking young men. Proud as a peacock, with grace and poise my darling niece climbed up on her bicycle, determined to have those fellows look her way. As she began her ride, she glanced over at the guys to see if her bait was doing the trick. Completely unaware, this babe immediately turned into pain and destruction. Parked just beyond her glancing eyes sat a big-wheeled monster truck. Without hesitation, she rammed right into the side of that stilled vehicle. Slinging her body over the handlebars, she quickly landed flat on her face. Sprawled out on the pavement from her ungraceful fall, the attention she was hopeful for was certainly received. The boys were so consumed in hysterical laughter that the poor dear couldn't even get anyone to help her up. Doubled over laughing, we finally got our wits about us to make sure my dear niece had no broken bones or serious cuts or bruises. Fortunately, the only thing that was hurt was her pride.

How many times in life do we do the same? We get preoccupied with trying to please someone or show off to another when we should be paying attention to the road ahead. Because our focus is wavered our direction is rapidly detoured. Unlike my niece's captivated audience, fortunately God never stops to react. He is always there, just in time to help us up. He is always eager to make sure to dust us off and get us back on track.

What is it today that has your attention? What is it that has taken your focus from the ride? Take a minute and re-evaluate your way. Allow God to be your focus and your guide.

*"So then, let us not be like others, who are asleep,*
*but let us be awake and sober."*
*1 Thessalonians 5:6 (NIV)*

# THY ROD

From 1984 to 2003 my mom has served as Chair for the North Georgia Walk to Emmaus. Preparing for board meetings, articles for printing, and her service for their spiritual weekends, mom spent several weeks in advance researching and praying for guidance. Like every other time, mom trusted in God's wisdom to provide that essential verse she would need to build on and fashion the theme around for the weekend. Eventually, God did give her a verse. This one particular time it was Psalm 23. Somewhat surprised and unable to correlate her lesson with this particular scripture, God continued to whisper it to her over and over again. *"Thy rod and thy staff shall comfort me"* permeated her spirit!

In May of 2001, just a few weeks prior to her weekend retreat, both my parents were involved in a major interstate accident. Heading north, they were hit head on by a speeding car that lost control in the southbound lane. Upon impact, the passenger seat, holding my mom, cracked literally in half. In the course of the impact her right leg was severely broken. After being rushed to the ER by ambulance, x-rays confirmed the severity of her break. Mom was quickly rushed to the operating room. In order to repair the damage caused, she received a steel rod to support and repair the broken bones in her leg.

As she lay in the hospital bed bruised, cut and sore from the accident, the Lord again whispered those same comforting words. *"Thy rod and thy staff shall comfort me."* God knew weeks before that she would need His peace. Knowing the upcoming trauma she would endure from the accident, He intentionally prepared her heart for the trust He knew she would eventually require of Him. While her leg contained her own personal rod, God used it to continually remind her of His provision and promise found in His trustworthy Word.

Today my mom has healed. She still holds the verse God gave her that day very dear to her heart. Knowing that God goes before us in all that we encounter in life, my mom is assured she doesn't have to worry. She is certain God can and will guide, watch over and prepare her no matter the circumstance!

What about you? Has God whispered to you lately? Have you chosen to tuck His Words down deep, or ignore His gentle voice? Take time today to hear from the Father. Take time today to digest His Holy Word.

*"Your rod and your staff, they comfort me."*
*Psalm 23:4b (NIV)*

# THE SOUND OF LAUGHTER

*I* absolutely love to laugh. Not only does it make me feel better inside, but I understand it's also good exercise. Those of you who know me well know that I'll do just about anything to avoid having to exercise but if laughter will help shed a few pounds, I'm all for it!

Over the years I have met many people but only one I consider the funniest. She was my best friend and adopted little sister. She could always make me laugh. The best part was even in the middle of a major crisis she would cut up if she knew it would heal the wound!

One of those times was a hot summer day in July. My grandmother and aunt had come to visit for the week and our pool was finally open. Now if I'd told my children once, I'd told them one hundred times not to come in the back door with wet feet. It would be a tragic event if someone were to fall and break a leg!

This particular day, the grill was fired up, the hot dogs and hamburgers were finally ready and of course, everyone was starving. As I opened the back door with the plate of hot food in hand, I suddenly gave way to the biggest fall you have ever seen. Hot dogs, hamburgers and me instantaneously flew into the air and landing on that wet linoleum floor, my legs began to sting from the fresh branding of several of those dogs.

As my considerate little sister helped me up, no amount of anger could have possibly outweighed the hilarious site of my non-acrobatic moves. Fortunately, I was spared from the earlier prediction of a broken leg. My children, however, knew mom meant business from that moment on.

Sometimes, God, too, wants us to simply laugh at ourselves. No matter if it's our fault or the one we have so often warned. Many times we have to get up, compose ourselves and then gracefully take a bow. God, too, will often lend us a friend who will kindly help us find humor even in a mess.

Take time today to laugh about your past. Take time to thank God for that funny friend He has sent you to help cope along the way. Thank Him even more for the gift of laughter that will ease the pain and magnify the joy in all the events of our lives!

*"A happy heart makes the face cheerful."*
*Proverbs 15:13a (NIV)*

# A TENNESSEE SEPTEMBER

It was a cool September afternoon. I was driving home from an errand I had run. I took the scenic route on a very narrow country road. My two, then little girls were in the backseat when we noticed a barn straight ahead. Strangely, there was smoke escaping from its roof. Knowing I had to alert the barn owner that their barn was on fire, I immediately turned into the driveway beside of it. After knocking and knocking on the homeowner's door, I realized no one was home. I looked around and noticed a neighbor's house just up the hill. I flew up their driveway hoping I'd be in time before the entire barn was up in flames. Slamming the car door, I proceeded to their front door knocking and hoping someone would answer. While I waited, I just happened to glance over the hill behind their house to only discover another smoking barn. Immediately I realized what an idiot I was. The barn wasn't on fire. They were smoking tobacco!

Growing up a Georgia girl, smoking tobacco barns were not something I was familiar with at all. When I shared my discovery with the homeowner, we laughed together and still chuckling at myself, I got back in the car. I can tell you though, this wouldn't be the last knock experienced by a tobacco burning barn owner in Tennessee. I'm certain another naive soul like me will surely bite the bait of escaping smoke!

I also knew this would be an excellent time to share a valuable piece of information about smoking barns with both my girls. This talk would save them the sheer embarrassment I had just experienced!

Isn't that just like God? He will go before us, check out the surroundings and take on the embarrassment of our mistakes. Even at that, He will gently give us pointers for our understanding in the future.

What about you? Has God ever gone before you? Has He taken on your embarrassments of life? Thank Him today for His willingness to love you, go before you, and never leave you alone!

*"God's wisdom is something mysterious that goes deep into the interior of His purposes.*
*You don't find it lying around on the surface. It's not the latest message, but*
*more like the oldest—what God determined as the way to bring out*
*His best in us, long before we ever arrived on the scene."*
*1 Corinthians 2:7 (The Message)*

# GROOMING WITH THE TIMES

*W*hen God "called" me into youth ministry in 1996, there was no doubt in my mind of the "calling." The only doubt I did have was my qualifications, which was based on a man's perceived criteria. As I graveled within what a "woman" like me with no history of youth experience could give to a youth group, God quickly challenged my thinking. He took me back to my childhood where He began the grooming process.

When I was in the fourth grade, my grandfather was rushed to the hospital. I knew beyond a shadow of a doubt that he was about to pass away. He did that night. God revealed that was the gift of discernment. As a teenager in high school, all of my friends came to me for advice and counsel. God revealed He had instilled the gift of encourager within me. Throughout my adulthood years, the Lord sent person after person to me to share the good news of Jesus Christ. That was ministry! Having three children five and a half years apart created a revolving door of teens to minister to for many, many years. That was my main experience! All of my days, the Lord had very precisely worked in ways I hadn't even put together. He was using my obedience and the opportunities He set before me, as experience and qualification for me to be in full-time ministry. Isn't that what we're here for anyway? Doesn't He just want our obedience? Without it, we can never fulfill His plan for our lives.

Fortunately today, I am assured of the ministry God has called me to. Aware that He continues to teach, lead, guide, direct, purpose and prepare me, I am willing to go wherever He leads. Every year, I am confident of the direction He takes me. I am assured He uses me for His kingdom's glory!

Throughout your lifetime, how has God been grooming you and you didn't even realize it? Has He used you and is He preparing you for ways you never even imagined? Take time to walk back in time with the Master. Let Him show you where and how He has been specifically grooming and leading your life for His glory. Your life, my friend, just may unrepentantly change for the better!

*"Many are the plans in a person's heart,*
*but it is the Lord's purpose that prevails"*
*Proverbs 19:21 (NIV)*

# MISSING IN ACTION

*P*reparing for a week of church summer camp, my friend and I went into town to finish up some of the last minute details. It was just a few hours before we were scheduled to leave. Soon we'd meet at the church and tackle the trip with 128 eager campers! One of the errands was picking up the awards and plaques to be given out throughout the week. Parking the car, my friend and I talked about all the last minute details I still needed to complete. Like usual, when I have a million things on my mind, I got out of the car not really paying much attention to where I was walking. The distance between the car and the shop was only a short piece and there was no activity anywhere near the place. All of a sudden, walking up the sidewalk, I felt myself literally loose all control. Without warning, my leg slipped down an enormous manhole through a very poorly placed cap. Panicked, as best I could, I braced myself for the fall. Within seconds, I was sprawled out all over the sidewalk. One leg was in the hole and the rest of me was laying flat on the ground. Silently, I just laid there. I was totally in shock, not to mention severe pain! Up ahead, my friend was still talking as if I was right there beside her. Looking over, she finally realized I had disappeared. Quickly turning around, she witnessed all of me flatly positioned on the concrete sidewalk below. Laughing hysterically, she ran over to give me a hand. At that point, I was in way too much shock and pain, to even react to her unconcerned affection for my leg or me. Eventually I elevated myself from the ground. I stood up and hobbled slowly into the store. Still gathering myself as best I could, I tried to act as if everything was just fine. With all laughs aside and the pain set in, my trip to camp was now accompanied with a sprained leg and a slower pace. Some things you can just never avoid.

There are many mishaps that will hit us in life. Sometimes we will be totally blindsided. Other times, we can see things coming at us but we just can't stop them quickly enough. Perhaps God allows the mishaps to slow us down. Maybe He allows them to get our attention. And sometimes, He allows them because we ask that of Him. No matter, God is always there to help us up. He will be the hand that gently raises us from our falls. He will guide us to a safer place of refuge.

What is it today from which you need God to pick you up? What is it from which He can pull you out? Ask Him today, to rescue you. His hand is always ready to pull you up and stand you perfectly positioned on your feet.

*"Surely the arm of the Lord is not too short to*
*save, nor His ear too dull to hear,*
*Isaiah 59:1 (NIV)*

# ANOTHER'S MONEY IS BETTER

*I*n the summer of 1998, my husband, daughter, son, and adopted daughter accompanied me not only to participate in the weeklong activities but to help with the everyday responsibilities of running a camp for teens. The retreat center was in Panama City Beach, FL.

Every day from lunch to five o'clock was free time. Students and leaders had the opportunity to enjoy the beach, rest, visit, eat or prepare for the next sessions. Because of the responsibilities on my plate, most of my free time was preparing for future worship services and events.

My adopted daughter was very helpful and was usually involved with the other leaders and me preparing for the day ahead. With no need to spend any money, she put it in my purse for safekeeping. We were way too busy to shop. My daughter, on the other hand, purposed to shop, everyday! She would come to me and ask if she could borrow a few dollars and I'd just send her to get money from my wallet, which she gladly did. It was much easier for me to have her get the money than for me to take the time to hand it out.

At the end of the week, packing our suitcases to go home, I noticed that my daughter had quite a bit of extra items that she had not brought on the trip. Proudly, she showed me her new t-shirts, jewelry, hats, postcards and several other souvenirs to remember her trip. Immediately I was concerned. I knew the price tags on these items added up to quite a bit of money. Questing how she was able to afford all of her stuff, she quickly replied, "The money in your wallet mom." I was puzzled. I knew I had not brought much money, especially not enough to buy her a suitcase full of new items. Suddenly, I remembered that my adopted daughter had stowed her money in my purse. Questioning where she had stored her money she replied, "In your wallet with your money." Immediately I knew where the money had come from. It was not my money but my adopted daughter's she had spent!

Fortunately, some of the items were returnable and the others, well I had to pay for them with my money. It was a tough lesson learned for all of us. Needless to say, we laughed and laughed. To this day my daughter still reaps the consequences of her spending spree with another's money!

What about you? Have you ever been put in a situation where you assumed you were doing right to find out you were really wrong? Have you had to reap the consequences of your actions? Take time today to thank God that, unlike us, He accepts our apology and never mentions the situation again. His forgiveness comes with a 100% guarantee of forgetfulness. Examine your heart and realize the comfort we have in a God who loves us unconditionally, no matter what we do or get ourselves into. He is always there to lead us out, the easy way!

*"Blessed are they whose transgressions are forgiven,*
*whose sins are covered. Blessed is the one whose sin*
*the Lord will never count against him."*
*Romans 4: 7-8 (NIV)*

# RUN THE RACE

*I*n June of 1998, 128 young people and adults boarded buses for a week of summer camp. Beginning in January of that same year, the leadership team fervently spent hundreds of hours of preparation and hard labor to bring this event together. On our knees, God met us with our every need and knew the name of every soul that was to eventually load that bus.

The week was one I can't adequately describe in words. Lives were changed, hopes were raised, and God's Spirit blanketed every event. As it drew to a close, the teens were challenged to *"Run The Race."* There on the beach in Panama City, 90 young people individually ran across the starting line passing off a baton to the next person to run. Each individual ran with all of their might in that heavy, deep sand but, each one knew that God was the true wind beneath their wings. A baton was given to every runner that day as a reminder of his or her race. Occasionally, I wonder about each of those batons. Are they shoved in a drawer, displayed as a reminder, or tossed in the trash? Regardless, that memory is still embedded within every heart.

This life calls for all of us to *"Run The Race"* even when the running gets tough. We must all know that once in a while, the sand will trip us up, or quickly suck us in. Although our steps may be tossed and turned, the waves of time will eventually wash us ashore. There on the beach, the tide will subside and God stands patiently awaiting our cry.

Nearly fourteen years have pasted and only God knows if each individual is still running that race. Some have passed away, some have walked away and the remainder have stayed the course. Only God can see who has chosen to stay in the race and also those who have let go and fell out of the race. I am assured however, that one fine day, God will whisper each name, like that day on the beach. I know that He will walk out into the deep and faithfully lead that lost sheep home.

What about you? Do you hear Him calling today? Take time to evaluate the path you are on. Allow God to meet you at that very place and restore, renew, redo or perhaps revive your desire and commitment to serve Him completely.

> *"Let us **RUN** with endurance **THE RACE** that is set before us,*
> *looking unto Jesus, the author and finisher of our faith."*
> *Hebrews 12:2 (NKJV)*

# HONORABLE BRAVERY

*M*y husband's grandmother was an amazing woman. When the two of us started dating, he took me to meet her in his hometown of Tallapoosa, GA. I instantly fell in love with her. MaMa Langley was her name.

Her homestead was on a corner lot just outside of town adorned with rockers on the front porch and a garden in the back. She found time to do all that was needed to be done in a day. Her husband passed away a few years earlier so the house was then hers to care for.

One day when we were visiting, we sat on the porch and just talked. She shared an amazing story about her week. The day before, she sighted a rattlesnake in her yard. (I think with the garden, this was somewhat common.) Certainly not having the likes of a snake on her property, she proceeded to get her garden hoe and without hesitation she chopped off its head! Quickly, and without hesitation, she ended the life of that pest of a snake. The ridiculous part was that this was not a small snake. He had fourteen rattlers and was over six feet long! She didn't even flinch. She just said, "'Ya gotta do what 'ya gotta do sometimes!" I knew then, nothing could stop this woman!

Spending time with her, throughout the years taught me a lot about survival. She shared with me her stories of growing up a country girl and living on the farm. Her life was interesting to me because I saw so much of what she was taught bleed from her being. I admired her strength and will to live life no matter the circumstance!

God teaches us, too, through His Word. He lays out instruction after instruction when we are left to do things on our own. Unlike MaMa Langley after her husband died, God never leaves us. He promises to guide and direct our paths and shows us what we need to do through obedience to His Word. It's in that obedience that we can experience the joy of our salvation. We too can live life with the comfort that we have a Father that will always be beside us no matter our circumstances.

What about you? Do you know God as your Comforter, Guide and Father? Take time today to evaluate your life. Take time to make sure you have the hope of a Savior that lives to see you through any situation you will ever face on earth!

*"Though I scatter them among the peoples, yet in distant lands they will remember*
*me. They and their children will survive, and they will return."*
*Zechariah 10:9 (NIV)*

# DETERMINATION DRIVES

$\mathcal{M}$y middle daughter was in the fifth grade when this particular summer, her and a few of her friends went to the park to enjoy "Bike Safety Day" sponsored by our city. This was a yearly event that included games, food, entertainment, and safety courses for all aspects of life. She loved going to the park any chance she got.

One of the greatest qualities my daughter is blessed with is persistence and determination. When she sets her mind to something it takes an act of congress for her to change it. This day was no exception!

The city hosted several give-a-ways and one was a girl's ten-speed bicycle. When my daughter saw that bike, she was determined to win it. As part of her strategy, she filled out not only one entry card but several. Fifty would probably be an accurate guess. She stayed at the park all day next to the bike. She made friends with the officer that was in charge of guarding the bike. She even dreamed of where she'd ride that bike! All day long, she waited. She waited and waited. Finally, after most of the other parkgoers had gone home, it was time to draw the name of the lucky winner. Poised and ready to take her prize home, my daughter anxiously awaited her name to be called. Reaching in and pulling out the new owners name was the officer on guard. "The winner of the brand new girl's 10-speed bicycle is. . . . . . ." Jumping higher than she's ever jumped, screaming louder than she's ever screamed, my baby girl heard her name. She was the winner of the bike she had dreamed of all day long! Her wait, her persistence and her determination to stay with it until the end was worth it all!

Driving up in her friend's daddy's truck, I could hear her screaming my name. Walking outside, there she proudly stood with her bike in hand. She was grinning from ear to ear. Her joy was indescribable. Her excitement was certainly in high gear. She was a winner and no one could take that away from her!

Like my daughter, God has given us opportunity after opportunity to walk in obedience and receive the greatest of rewards. Loving us unconditionally, He knows walking in His ways will surely prevent unwanted misfortunes and situations in our life. By honoring His Word, blessings are guaranteed instead of curses.

Take time today to evaluate where you are going. Are you listening, depending and waiting on God or are you heading in the opposite direction? Stop today and question your motives. Make certain you are moving in the direction of blessings instead of curses. God wants the best for you in every single way!

*"If you do whatever I command you and walk in obedience to me and do what is right in*
*my eyes by keeping my decrees and commands, as David my servant did, I will be with you.*
*I will build you a dynasty as enduring as the one I built for David and will give Israel to you."*
*1 Kings 11:38 (NIV)*

# OUR GIRLY GIRL

My baby girl was most assuredly a girly girl! She squealed, screamed and talked constantly. She was an entertainer and one of the happiest little girl's I knew. She was always hanging with the little neighborhood girls outside and it was obvious she wanted to be a cheerleader! She began cheering at an early age and cheered about everything.

When she went to kindergarten, one of the speech teachers contacted me about her voice being raspy. Like most mothers, I immediately became defensive. I didn't want to believe anything was wrong with her and I found myself a bit angry that this stranger had even mentioned anything. She was convinced my daughter had nodules on her vocal chords and would never be able to cheer. Calming myself down, I agreed to have her checked out.

As recommended, we went to see an ear, nose and throat doctor. In order to see if the teacher's suspicions were correct, the doctor sat her in the lap of the male nurse, sprayed her nose and as the nurse held her down, the doctor forced tubes into her nostrils and throat. Of course my daughter was screaming and struggling to free herself. I was livid! Having no forewarning of this type of traumatic procedure, we were not prepared. As my baby struggled, I wanted to scream at the doctor to stop hurting her and release her! The entire experience was infuriating and an all around nightmare! Returning to the school, I reported the physician's actions and announced my refusal to take her back. The therapist agreed and made us aware that if my daughter did not scream for a while, the nodules would disappear on their own and she would maybe one day cheer again. Still angry, I was furious this had not been suggested from the start! If it had been, this horrifying event would have been prevented!

Fortunately, my daughter followed the therapist's instructions and worked very hard not to scream. Because of it, her nodules disappeared and she was indeed able to cheer. Not only did she cheer her entire high school years, but served as the Captain of the Cheer Squad her senior year! Following simple directions and much prayer, she was able to be what she knew God intended for her to be!

God loves cheerleaders. In fact, He is one. He cheers us on! No matter what age in life, what situation in life or what place in life, He is there. He has promised to stay with us telling us the things we do not know that can and will direct our future in a successful and positive way!

What about you? Have you given your life to Christ so that He can be your permanent cheerleader? Have you realized without Him you can do nothing? Take time today to make sure you have Him on your team. Make sure He is the one you can call on and He will be there to cheer you on!

*"If any of you lacks wisdom, you should ask God,*
*who gives generously to all without finding*
*fault, and it will be given to you"*
*James 1:5 (NLT)*

# MOMMA KNOWS

For the first time as a teen we reluctantly left our son home for the weekend as the rest of the family went out of town. Running over the rules and trying not to portray the distrust in our voices, my husband and I strove to anticipate positive results upon our return.

Like most parents would do once the weekend was over I immediately looked for any evidence that would tell the tale of the activity while we were away. Sure enough, I found it. In the bonus room the furniture was neatly in place (at least to most) but as I investigated every piece was moved about an inch to the right of it's original position. The indented weight marks in the carpet proved it. Questioning my son's mysterious activities, he admitted to wrestling with a buddy. Not convinced, I waited for the rest to surface. Sure enough it did, later in the week at the checkout counter of a local grocery store. A sweet young woman I knew apologized to me for not being able to attend my son's apparent gathering at our house. In fact, she had no idea that I didn't know of his party planning. Playing along I assured her I would let my sweet boy know. Walking proudly just a few doors down the walkway to his place of employment, I quickly delivered the news of her regret. Dumbfounded as if he'd seen a ghost, I pleasingly announced my findings of his so-called non-eventful weekend activities.

It amazes me how somewhere buried within God has placed maternal instinct.

Without any classes or illustrations from a book some things are simply what we refer to as "gut feelings." When he was a young boy I constantly told my son that the best thing to do was tell the truth. Somehow, someway, momma would end up finding out the facts.

God, too, knows our activities. He created us. He knows us. He loves us and He is about us. Trying to "get away with" things may last for a moment but eventually our doings will be found out. The things we try so hard to keep secret, God already knows all about. In fact, He was there when it happened. He even knew what we were about to do before we did. It is in our best interest to simply trust God. When our sins have caught up with us and the evidence has surfaced we need to just take it to the Father. (and sometimes momma!) Confessing brings about cleansing and change of heart. The more we reason with the wait, the wait will reason with us. Letting go changes the circumstance and the outcome.

What is it that you need to take to the Father today? Do you live in regret and the weight of lies? Are you hiding from the sin that has somehow entangled you? Take time today to talk to your Creator. Trust Him to restore you this moment and clean up the remnants of your undesirable mess!

*"If we confess our sins, He is faithful and just and will forgive us
our sins and purify us from all unrighteousness."
1 John 1:9 (NIV)*

# PUZZLE PIECES

My mama always loved to work puzzles. Her favorites were the ones that had over 500 pieces. Although it may have taken a week or a month, she always finished what she started. Most of the time in between her daily duties, she made her way back to the table that hosted what seemed like millions of pieces! What was the most rewarding to her was completing the design! With each individual piece she would intently place each one exactly where if fit. With only a picture on the box top, to me it seemed impossible to make a matching picture with all those little cutout forms. With her eye and her drive to succeed, she would endlessly work and work and work until she completed the replica of the picture on the box. Then magically, laid out on her card table, was a successfully finished product solely from her mere determination.

As for me, I don't care too much for fitting puzzles together. Although I love a good challenge, it has to be one that interests me! The more pieces in a puzzle, the more difficult it seems. Instantly, it makes me anxious thinking I have to complete it. On the other hand, I experience boredom from the persistence it requires and I would just as soon walk away and quit than to antagonize over completing it!

It's amazing how God has created us so different. Even my mom and me, although we are so much alike in so many ways, in others we are complete opposites.

We, like puzzle pieces fit exactly where God places us. Some are large, some are small, some are colorful, and some are not. Some fit perfectly on top while others are positioned preciously in the middle. No matter where our piece fits, the puzzle is not complete without every single one. No matter our likes, dislikes or personality traits God has the exact spot we each are perfectly positioned!

The body of Christ is comparable to that of the big puzzle. God uses our gifts and talents to colorfully display a gorgeous scene. He concludes the final picture with our greatest qualities, and features them for all to see. Each individual is purposed as His handiwork has been recorded.

Where is it that you fit in God's picture of time? Have you allowed Him to carve you out fitting you perfectly in place? Ask Him today to lay before you your place in His Kingdom's work. Give Him charge of your life so that your best qualities will supersede your weaknesses to further enhance His Kingdom business!

*"Just as a body, though one, has many parts, but all its*
*many parts form one body, so it is with Christ."*
1 Corinthians 12:12 (NIV)

# COMFORT AND JOY

Gathering in the hair salon in the basement of her home, my two friends and I enjoyed the time, as girls will often do. One of those occasions ushered in a conversation, of all things, requiring the revealing of our once confidential bra sizes. Now I can admit very honestly that even at my then age of 40, I had never been to the local department store to be sized. In fact, I never even knew that was what women were supposed to do! You see, my great aunt worked for a popular bra company and would always provide us with much discontinued merchandise. For as long as I had lived, these bras had adorned my chest-of-drawers. Every shape, but only one certain size was available for our picking. The 34B that always seemed to fit me, managed to be my permanent choice.

As I proudly shared my bra size with my friends, with gaping mouths, they could not help but argue with my innocence. Of course after gaining weight from my slim figure in high school, was a dead give away to the bosoms I had now acquired! Finally, revealing my attire, they were intrigued at how I was even able to hook it around me. It was apparent to them that the excess skin that was falling out of the sides and the front of my brassiere was not suppose to be this way. To me, it was that acquired size I had taken ownership of several years back! Laughing uncontrollably, they directed me to the nearest department store for the ultimate test of cup sizes. Feeling somewhat clueless, sure enough, that day I graduated from a size B cup to a full figured D cup.

Today, I laugh and breathe in relief as I comfortably fit in my new wear. Still amazed at my lack of education, I think of how God loves that about me. I know, He too, must giggle at how I get so excited about learning something new. How childlike I remain sometimes and yet when I must grow up, I step out and find the greatness of a new and better way.

What about you? Has God laughed at you lately? Is there something in your innocent way you need to wake up to so that He may also lead you too much more comfort? Enjoy time today with your Father. Enjoy time laughing in the presence of your Lord.

*"See what great love the Father has lavished on us, that we*
*should be called children of God! And that is what we are!"*
*1 John 3:1 (NIV)*

# COLORFUL PAPER

*I*t was my 40th birthday and my husband made arrangements to take me to a wonderful restaurant in Nashville. Not only was the place delightful, but so was the surprise of our closest two couple friends who joined us for the evening's festivities. I was overjoyed they had come to celebrate on my account!

Dinner was fabulous and filled with great conversation and lots of friendly laughter. Amidst all of the food, one of my friends had so thoughtfully placed hundreds of pieces of fine confetti to adorn my birthday table. With hats, horns, gifts, confetti and my own birthday cake, the evening was a great success!

After dinner, the men agreed to drive the car around while we ladies gracefully walked the elegant staircase. I must add that in our classy dresses and fashionable coats, we looked divine! As we approached the entrance and the maître d' bid us farewell, my friend decided that the confetti was much too precious to waste. Slipping up beside me, she carefully dropped a hand-full into each pocket of my beautiful fashionable coat. Certainly unaware of the huge holes both my pockets contained, streams of confetti doused the floor underneath me. Totally caught off guard, my friend quickly howls with laughter. The echo of her cry rang through the foyer as all eyes turned to catch me in a pool of a billion tiny pieces of shiny colored paper. Like being frozen in time, I could feel every eye in that establishment glaring at the spectacle she had made of me!

Needless to say, I have never graced that eatery again. I do though, giggle with glee every time I remember it. I often think how so many times we as individuals will walk by in our dressy costumes to only hide the deterioration inside. The holes within are so humiliating but we dress our outside with colorful fashion to camouflage the affliction we really carry. God though, wants to sew us up. He wants to take those things that cause corrosion and flush our system out. He wants to take our holes and gently sew them up with the freshness of Himself.

What about you? Do you have holes in your internal garment? Take time today to talk to the Father. Take time today to let the master seamstress repair your earthly deterioration and troubles within.

*"Set your minds on things above, not on earthly things. For you*
*died, and your life is now hidden with Christ in God."*
*Colossians 3:2 &3 (NIV)*

# IT'S SAFE TO GO IN

*I*t was a Wednesday evening church night with choir practice following the service. In order to get my two daughters' in bed for school the next day, I asked my adopted daughter to take the girls home for me. She was glad to do so.

As the girl's arrived at home, my youngest opened the garage door to go inside. Forgetting the security system had been set the 60-second delay beeping began. As my adopted daughter came in to turn off the alarm, she realized she couldn't remember the code. Trying frantically to recall it, the alarm went off in full force. The sound was piercing and frightening for all of them. In no time, the local police department was in the front yard instructing the three to come outside. With their hands up, they sheepishly stepped onto the porch. Hoping to clear up any confusion, my adopted daughter explained that she was the babysitter and had just forgotten the code. Talking through the ordeal, the officer agreed to let the girls go back inside.

Just as the officer prepared to leave, my youngest ask if the officer would please go in and check to see if there were in burglars in the house. Taken back by her unbelievable question, my adopted daughter turned and said, "You were the one that set off the alarm in the first place." Realizing her error, they all chuckled and went back inside.

The rest of the evening, the girl's were a little rattled by the incident, but thankfully everything turned out all right. Memorizing the code was definitely on the agenda for future occurrences.

Like my youngest daughter, many times we too open the door to potential dangerous situations. Not aware of our surroundings or perhaps not paying attention to what's ahead, we barrel forward unprepared. In these unpredictable times, we need the help of a Savior. We need the one who can stand in the gap in our times of trouble.

What about you? Have you found yourself in the midst of a sticky situation? Have you gone ahead and now you need some direction? Allow God to have the lead. Allow the one who has the answers be your escort today.

*"The Lord makes firm the steps of the one who delights in Him;*
*though he may stumble, he will not fall, for the*
*Lord upholds him with his hand.*
*Psalm 37: 23 & 24 (NIV)*

# TO BREATHE OR NOT TO BREATHE

*S*uffering from Emphysema, my mother-in-law was forced to be put on oxygen. Whenever she went out of town, she carried small cylinders with her and a tank was delivered wherever she would travel.

This particular trip was to Nashville. Already visiting my parents' home in Georgia, I met her sister and picked her up. She rode to our house with me.

The trip home took about four hours. It was a great ride to talk and catch up on the things that had happened in our absence. Small town gossip, family situations and grandchildren were just a few of the items on our checklist! Arriving halfway in Chattanooga, we stopped at a rest area to stretch our legs and use the restroom. Deciding to go ahead and change out her oxygen tank, she reached in her travel bag. Frantic, she realized her extra tank was not there.

Sure enough, we had left it in her sister's car. Trying not to panic, she kept her mind on controlling her breathing and believing she could make it home. The trip continued to go well. Just outside of Nashville, her breathing was amazingly normal and it seemed her calm behavior had paid off. Next thing I knew, she asked me to stop again. Needing gas, I pulled off the interstate into a nearby service station. When my mother-in-law got out of the car, I was a little puzzled. She didn't need to go the restroom as I had suspected, she was ready to have a cigarette. I was in complete shock! Even without oxygen and a diagnosis of Emphysema, she was confident she would be fine. I filled my gas tank and we continued on our way to Nashville.

Sometimes life is just unpredictable. People are too! Habits, addictions, misconceptions, and our own stubbornness over-rule the reality of our current situation. Nevertheless, God wants us to know the truth. He wants to see us through if we are willing to allow Him to deal with our fleshly desires. His way is not to punish or control us. It's truly just the opposite. Because of His love for us, He knows that freedom lies in our obedience. Freedom from the chains that bind.

What about you? Have you something in your life that needs His divine attention? Do you live with a habit, a belief, a misconception or a stubborn mindset that has you all bound up? Come to the Father today. Allow Him to minister to your flesh and remove the chains that have imprisoned you. Take time today to thank God that He can and will set you free!

*"It is for freedom that Christ has set us free. Stand firm, then, and do*
*not let yourselves be burdened again by a yoke of slavery."*
*Galatians 5:1 (NIV)*

# HER BIRTH

*T*he evening of April 26, 2003 was a very special day in the history of my life. It was a day I never expected. God had continued to pour out His blessings on me and in doing so He had honored the fruits of my labor. Investing many hours in the lives of teenagers in the youth group I ministered to, God surprised me this day with an honorable blessing. The blessing came directly from one of those teens!

On this evening, a precious baby girl was born to a young man and his wife. This young man was like a son to my husband and me. The couple agreed to name their precious baby girl after me! Her father, upon the news of her conception, had written me a letter about his decision to name her "*Alicia*". I could barely believe his words. It's still hard to believe! I don't think I will ever be able to adequately express in words the honor of this event!

In the Old Testament, many prophets record the meanings of names and how God chooses them. I trust that as the Lord has blessed my life, and my name too, He will bless this new little life. My prayer was that she would also trust in the Lord as her comfort and shield. I prayed for her salvation and anointing in her daily walk. As I prayed this into her life on her birthday, at the age of six, indeed, Alicia accepted the Lord into her heart. She followed her decision by participating in Believer's Baptism. I again was honored to attend that special event. Like her father and mother, she is walking in the ways of her Lord and Savior, Jesus Christ!

Oh how majestic is your name, God. How wonderful you are to allow us to bask in your glory as you create new life. How awesome it is to see your handiwork as new life is formed and created. Oh God, it's not all about the names that we chose, but the life that you have created. May we be reminded that you have afforded us the opportunity to experience life, enjoy life, and share life with you from birth until death.

What about you? Have you experienced the joy of a new birth? Have you seen God's glory in the preciousness and newness of a baby boy or girl? Take time today to thank Him for His amazing creations. Take time today to relive that moment in your own life.

> *"A good name is more desirable than great riches;*
> *to be esteemed is better than silver or gold."*
> *Proverbs 22:1 (NIV)*

# MY TREASURE BOX

As far back as my elementary days, I can remember dreaming of the day I would marry. I can recall being so excited about meeting the man of my dreams and sharing my life with him. I can also remember the thrill of thinking about having children. Making up names and looking forward to seeing their tiny faces always stirred my soul!

To prepare for that day I would marry my prince charming, my parents gave me my very own wooden hope chest. Positioning it at the foot of my bed, I began preparing for that magical day! Filling it with items I would eventually use when I married was such an adventure for me. From dishes to a can opener, that chest would one day overflow with just enough possessions to begin my new life. Many times I remember going through that chest to remind myself of what I had already gathered. Other times, I'd go through it to simply take inventory and see what else was needed to complete my collection!

Now in my late 50's, I have for several years started a new chest of sorts. I now have my treasure box for heaven. I have discovered that as we store up treasures such as our kindness, goodness, obedience, and thoughtfulness towards others, we are rewarded in Heaven. Although we may not be able to take our earthly possessions, we can take souls where we have faithfully planted seeds of faith. Over the years, God will nudge us to say a kind word. He may use us to speak truth into a gloomy situation. God may also have us be a shoulder for someone who so desperately needs us to gather his or her tears, extend a listening ear or a give a loving hug. I have also realized that all those tasks God assigned me to would not only bless the receiver, but also me. In my obedience, God has allowed a multitude of joy and fulfillment to come my way and the way of the one He placed before me.

From my earthly hope chest to my heavenly treasure box, I thank God for His blessings. Today I strive to fill up my box more than ever before. Today I wait in great anticipation for God to give me my next life-changing assignment. More than ever before, I long to be the hands and feet of Jesus for those He so desperately wants to touch!

Are there treasures in your box? If not, ask God what you can do for Him today. You will one day be amazed as He hands out the treasure the two of you have stored!

> *"And you will be blessed. Although they cannot repay you,*
> *you will be repaid at the resurrection of the righteous."*
> *Luke 14:14 (NIV)*

# CHARACTER CARVING

*B*eing a mom is one career that exhilarates almost every human emotion possible. With every single birth, I was never able to adequately find the words to describe the love God released within me. Seeing their precious little beings completely convinced me of the true awesomeness of our God!

Throughout our children's lives though, we have been fortunate enough to have them as character builders. What I mean is, every emotion known to man is pressed, pushed, engaged, erupted, evolved and secreted from our innermost parts by these little ones. As God individually knitted each child of mine differently He, too, used them in various ways in His process of perfecting me.

One was the sandpaper that consistently rubbed my imperfections. While I often tried to resist, I had to endure the pain of the sanding from my eldest daughter. As time went on and she grew to be a young woman, my heart eventually healed due to the effects of that sanding.

The other child was yet another builder. She knew just when enough was enough. Faithfully, she was always there to clean up shavings from what the other had left behind. While God continually perfected me, He knew I would need the sandpaper and the cleaner alike. One could not work without the other. The two went hand in hand!

As the carpenter creates his workmanship, the saw details every cut. The shavings remain as evidence of what use to be a part of the original piece. For the finished product to be complete, one of the requirements is the removal of all the imperfect pieces.

Although I'm still in the carving stage of me, the completion is somewhat near. The cuts have engraved a lasting effect towards the beauty of who I am. The shavings all around are constant reminders of where I was, how far I have come and what God has done for me.

Oh how God loves me. Oh how He, too, loves my children. I thank Him today for the character builders He has given me. Although I am still a work still in progress, I'm a masterpiece He'll completely perfect.

What character carvings have your children given you to date? What stage of the carving are you in? Have you seen the evidence of your perfection or are you still a work in progress? Thank God today for the refined product He wants you to be and thank Him for seeing you just like Him!

> *"Yet You, Lord, are our Father. We are the clay, you are*
> *the potter; we are all the work of your hand."*
> *Isaiah 64:8 (NIV)*

# A DIFFERENT MISSION

*B*eing the Minister of Students at a local Christian School in White House, TN, part of my job description was to plan and direct yearly three-day spiritual retreats. This particular year, the Head Master wanted to take steps to implement what the previous retreats had imparted in the hearts of the student body. Stepping into a new realm of ministry, some of the students were about to take their first mission trip.

Thirty-six junior and senior class members loaded the school bus headed to Lynch, KY. The weekend was to include helping local residents and non-profit business owners. Restoring a home that was a step away from being condemned, as well as cleaning and preparing a building for the opening of a community teen center were assignments on their agenda.

Arriving just after dark, the Head Master made an announcement that required an extreme amount of discipline from the students as well as the teachers. We were all instructed not to talk! I can just tell you I was speechless! My passion is talking! Being on staff, I had to suck it up and trust the Lord big time!

The exercise forced us to be quiet in our environment while enhancing our ability to hear God speak. That it did. Keeping silent all night, through breakfast and then on a morning walk was intense. Still silent, everyone followed our Head Master as he led us to a local apartment complex. Standing in the midst of all the onlookers was quite sobering. Awaiting further instruction, our leader scanned the area, reached over in the grass to pick up a discarded soda can. He immediately tossed the can in the trash. Within seconds, another person looked around, picked up some trash and tossed it in the trash basket. Without hesitation, every student and teacher alike joined in on the cleanup. Not one word was spoken. The onlookers just watched in amazement as our group selflessly cleaned their neighborhood.

As we returned to our quarters, we processed what we had just experienced. Our Head Master finally broke the silence. "I did not give you any instructions just now. You simply watched me. Without hesitation, you followed my leading. You made a difference. Now, I want you to think about those people around you in your everyday life. They are watching you too. What kind of difference are you making in their lives?"

Completely taken back, we all realized what a difference we do make even in the smallest of things. God uses each of us to change another's life. Whether He calls us to teach, listen, speak or not, He uses us.

What is it God is doing in and around you? Have you been obedient to make a positive difference or a negative one? Take time to evaluate your influence. Take time to see the ministry God has chosen specifically for you!

*"For you are a people holy to the Lord your God. The Lord your*
*God has chosen you out of all the peoples on the face of the*
*earth to be His people, His treasured possession."*
*Deuteronomy 7:6 (NIV)*

# DOWN HILL, OR NOT!

*I* had never seen so much snow in all of my life! Growing up in Georgia and living in Tennessee, from time to time we had a few inches of the "white stuff," but nothing like what we were seeing.

Two other couple friends, besides my husband and I, took a weeklong trip to Lake Tahoe, Nevada. It was winter at the time and there was at least twelve feet of snow. Skiing was on the agenda, of course, but it wasn't really all that appealing to one of my girl friends or me. Neither of us had ever skied before and we weren't so sure about learning. Getting to the ski lodge, covered up like two Eskimos, the two of us prepared to take on a new learning experience. The others, schooled in the sport, took the lift up the mountain and left us with our new skilled instructor.

Now walking in those long overrated skis was one thing, trying to actually ski on them was another. Standing on the "bunny slope," the beginner's hill was a little embarrassing when you were in the midst of nothing but a slew of younger girls and boys. Their skills were clearly much better than ours! Once the instruction was given, those kids began to ski down the slopes like pros! I, however, skied using my backside most of the time. My friend and I, well let's just say, needed a little more learning than just one lesson!

Not only did the weight of those skis make it hard to stand, our ankles were literally killing us walking in them. The whole experience was exhausting for both of us! Not quite as enthusiastic about the adventure as our other four friends, the two of us slung off our skis and quickly returned to the lodge for some warm hot chocolate and great conversation!

Often, as beginners, we don't see the true beauty that exists. Afraid to take a chance and step out into the unknown, we give up when the going gets rough. Although we may seem content, it's not until we climb to the top of our mountain experiences that we see the real view, the beauty in our adventure!

What about you? Have you chosen to forego the falls and remain in the simple life in the lodge, or are you willing to take a chance and climb the mountain while reaching your greatest potential? Take time to evaluate where you are today. Take time to know exactly where you want to go and how you want to get there. With God as your guide, He will allow you the choice and mark the road ahead. He alone is the one you need to allow you a clear path to stand and move forward.

*"Have I not commanded you? Be strong and courageous.*
*Do not be afraid; do not be discouraged, for the*
*Lord your God will be with you wherever you go."*
*Joshua 1:9 (NIV)*

# THE COLORED BOW

The fourth of July had become a traditional gathering at our house. Swimming, sunbathing, and relaxing were necessities on this day! Coupled with friends and family, usually 30 or more of us gathered later in the afternoon for a barbecue. After dark, from my back lawn, we all watched the most spectacular fireworks display from the city park. Every year was even better than the one before. This year was no exception!

Knowing my oldest daughter's birthday, July 22nd, would not be quiet as easy to round up all of her friends, we decided to surprise her on this special holiday. Her seventeenth birthday would bring in the car of her dreams. Picking it out weeks before, her dad tricked her into thinking it was not a good buy and he was therefore not purchasing it. Instead, her father bought the car, had the air-conditioner repaired and even added a brand new CD player.

After all of the guests had arrived, it was time for the surprise! With the music blaring, her dad and brother drove into the driveway in her new car. As my daughter turned around to see who had arrived, she caught sight of the humongous red bow on the hood of the car. Screaming, "My car! My car!", my daughter ran to hug her dad and thank him for her gift. The vehicle she had so hoped for was finally hers! It was truly the best birthday present ever!

I will never forget the expression of disbelief on our daughter's face. Her excitement melted the hearts of her dad and me. Filled with overwhelming joy, my grown up little girl was experiencing one of the most exciting times in her life! The car of her dreams had finally become reality.

God does have a way of allowing our dreams to materialize. Faithfully, He places special people in our lives, such as parents or friends. Because of the love we possess for one another, we are able to provide the dream and are in turn, blessed.

Have you had a dream God has fulfilled? Have you a desire you haven't asked of the Lord? Go to the Father today. Thank Him for allowing those in your life that will fulfill the dreams you so desire. Thank Him today for understanding your wants and needs, and according to His will, making them come true!

*"Hope deferred makes the heart sick,*
*but a longing fulfilled is a tree of life."*
*Proverbs 13:12 (NIV)*

# CARNATIONS

From a young age, I have had the gift of discernment. For many years I didn't understand how I knew things, but I knew that I knew them. I would suddenly have an inkling of something before it even occurred. I also couldn't understand how words would just flow from my lips and I had no way of knowing what I was saying. Finally as an adult, I realized this gift was from God. I don't know why, I was just thankful He gave it to me.

Several years ago, I was in my computer room paying bills and searching the web. Without any warning, I smelled carnations as if someone had placed them in front of my nose. I instantly turned to look to see if anyone had walked into the room. No one was there. I walked down the hall and no one had even come up the stairs. Sitting back down at my desk, I began smelling them again. I was puzzled. I knew that there was no trace of flowers but how could the smell be so real? Carnations are not one of my favorites either. In fact, I can't stand the smell of them.

Being around death all of my life did it. The smell immediately reminds me of a funeral home! In my spirit, I knew smelling carnations must also be related to a funeral. I felt like it was going to be one of our family members. Trying to forget, I refused to even allow myself to think about what had happened. Sure enough, the following week my husband's 21-year-old niece was killed in a car accident. I was beside myself.

A year later, again I was sitting at my computer and the same thing happened, the same smell, the same feeling and the same inkling engulfed me. I knew another death was about to occur, I just didn't know who or when. Unlike the time before though, I also saw in a vision the funeral home and people who have gathered there to pay their respects. Unfortunately, a week later, my mother-in-law unexpectedly passed away. To try to understand why God chose to warn me beforehand is impossible. He just did. I do think He knew the shock would be overbearing for me.

Life is filled with unpredictable and unexplainable events. Some things are to our advantage to know and others are not. God created us, knows our fears, our shortcomings and our reactions. Because of this, I believe He loves us enough to pad our falls. I am so grateful for His provision.

What about you? Do you trust God to take care of you when you are at your weakest? Do you perhaps trust Him to know your weaknesses even when you don't? Thank Him today for loving us enough to take care of our needs long before we know we need Him. Thank Him also for caring for you in any situation life may bring your way.

*"You are my hiding place; you will protect me from*
*trouble and surround me with songs of deliverance.*
*I will instruct and teach you in the way you should go;*
*I will counsel you with my loving eye on you."*
*Psalm 32:7 & 8 (NIV)*

# HER LAST BREATHS

*I*n the last few years of my mother in laws life, she developed Emphysema. She was put on oxygen permanently and she slowed down quite a bit. Even with her disease, she was unable to quit smoking. She just removed her oxygen, stepped on her front porch and smoked.

Still able to drive, she only traveled close to home. One day while driving to the store, my mother-in-law ran off the road. Trying to bring her car back onto the main road, she lost control of the car. She drove across the other lane, off into the woods and straight into a tree. Fortunately no one was in the opposite lane! Thankfully, the driver behind her alerted a rescue team by dialing 911.

When my mother-in-law arrived at the hospital, her oldest son and wife, whom she lived with, greeted her there. The hospital staff assured them she would be fine so they went home to gather her things and prepare for her to stay there for a few days.

My husband's mother had been a widow for 22 years. Her oldest son had recently been diagnosed with a fatal lung disease. She had worried herself crazy that the Lord would not allow her to die before her son. Watching her baby sister bury her child, she was fearful she would have to experience the same. "It just isn't natural," is what she'd say.

Before my brother-in-law and sister-in-law finished gathering her things at home, the hospital called. Her internal injuries were much more severe than they had anticipated. They were not optimistic about her survival. In complete shock, they returned to her side.

Traveling out of town, my husband could not make the trip to be with her until the next morning. Being the director of a school talent show, I could not leave until after the production. We both just prayed she would hold on long enough for my husband to go be with her.

The following morning, her baby son caught a flight and arrived at the hospital. I was on my way driving with the children. Hanging on with everything in her, my husband went into her room. They embraced, told one another they loved each other and just loved on one another for the next few minutes. Within about five minutes, my dear mother-in-law took her last breath. God heard her prayers. He not only took her before her oldest son passed away, but He brought her baby son before she stepped into eternity.

God hears our prayers. He knows our greatest desires. He is there to comfort us and be our everything. What about your life? Is He God of all? Are there desires you need to ask of Him? Are there areas in your life you need to offer Him full control? Take time today to evaluate your situations. Take time to inventory where He needs to indwell and become the center of your life.

*"Praise be to the God and Father of our Lord Jesus Christ,*
*the Father of compassion and the God of all comfort, who comforts*
*us in all our troubles, so that we can comfort those in any trouble*
*with the comfort we ourselves received from God."*
*2 Corinthians 1:3-4 (NIV)*

# WHO WOULD HE CHANGE?

*R*aised with a Christian heritage, my husband and I both agreed to lay the same foundation for our three children. Not only a faith-based home, but also good morals and values were essential.

Our middle child, however, somehow found a way to push the envelope as much as possible. She had her way of believing and her own way of wanting to do things. One of those things was her selection of boyfriends.

One particular boyfriend was two years younger than her. Most everything we preached against in a boy, she turned to. He was not a good influence. He was disrespectful to her and continued to walk with her down a destructive path. His upbringing was completely opposite than hers and therefore, caused much friction between her, her dad and me. Feeling like this young man was taking my daughter from me, I felt extreme resentment towards him. Every time we caught her in another lie, I disliked him more. Eventually, I have to admit, I hated him!

One evening, she begged for my husband and I to allow this young man to come to our home and talk. She was determined to be with him and strangely, she wanted our approval. Finally agreeing to her request, we invited him over. After my husband set the ground rules for their courtship, I set mine. I proudly told him that our daughter had been raised in a Christian home and that would be adhered to by both of them. They would be expected to follow what rules were set with no exceptions.

That night, I proudly prayed that the Lord change this young man's heart. I asked God to make him see things my way or change my heart. In a few weeks, I could see how God was going to answer my prayer. He was changing me. What the Lord spoke to me that night changed my life. He said, *"Alicia, you have ministered to all kinds of youth with issues just like this young man. Who do you think you are not allowing him to belong to your family? Are you too good for him?"* Speechless and ashamed, I realized the pride I possessed. I knew that God had different plans for him and me. In the days following, God provided opportunity after opportunity for me to minister to him. My heart was broken and this young man became like my own son. God knew that he needed me in his life as much as I needed him.

What about you? Has God lead someone in your life you have not welcomed? Has He sent someone your way that you've rejected? Think back, look around and see whom God may have purposed in your life that you turned away. Ask Him today to reveal whom you need to welcome with open arms.

*"Let the words of my mouth and the meditation of*
*my heart be acceptable in thy sight, O Lord,*
*my strength and my Redeemer."*
*Psalm 19:14 (KJV)*

# PROVISION AT IT'S BEST

*P*lanning, preparing, and directing three day retreats for middle and high school students required a great deal of creativity. As a part of the planning process, I recruited several students to perform skits and readings throughout the three-day event. Adding much needed flavor to any session, serious or not, is a must. So drama was just the perfect ingredient!

Because the school did not offer a yearly drama class, I approached the principal at the Christian school where I taught about considering providing it for the upcoming school year. Not only could skits be performed at the annual retreats each year, but chapel services as well. Loving my idea, he said, "Great! You can teach it!" Completely taken off guard I certainly was not going to turn down the challenge so I accepted. It was not until I recovered from shock that I realized I had no idea how or what I would do to teach this class. I was simply making a suggestion. I never dreamed I'd be the one to implement and teach it!

While the summer break progressed, my prayers did too. Actively seeking wisdom from the Lord, one day He spoke. "*What do today's teens watch more than anything,*" He asked. "Music videos," I replied. As clear as a bell the Lord said to me, "*Most all teens are dramatic. If you will search for the songs, I will not only give you a vision for a music video, but I will provide the students to edit the work.*" Completely floored, I knew He was a genius! (no pun intended) It was a perfect idea! There would be no memorization involved, which would attract more students and create their interest in participating in the class! Listening to all the music I could possibly find, God faithfully provided the songs and the visions needed to begin my course in the fall.

When the semester started, so did a one-of-a-kind drama class. The students were pumped and ready to make the vision God had given me come to life. Not only did the performers fit every part perfectly, but God lined up the exact shooting locations as well. From hospital emergency rooms to the use of fire trucks and ambulances; funeral homes to a cemetery; The Rescue Mission to back alleys; public schools to a court room. God had it all covered. We never paid a penny. Local business owners and public service people gladly provided our needs for FREE!

Unsure of my abilities, God was certain. Accepting the challenge, He was faithful to provide and bring out His best in me. Knowing nothing about the industry, He provided all I needed. All He needed was my submission. Through Him, I was blessed beyond measure. Through me, God proved who He really is when we let go and let Him.

What about you? Has God set you up to work through you? Has He called on you to work on His behalf? Take time today to recognize where God may be purposing to use you to accomplish the unknown. Take time to be willing to allow Him His way with you. Have Faith!

> *"I took you from the ends of the earth, from its farthest corners*
> *I called you. I said, 'You are my servant; I have chosen you*
> *and have not rejected you."*
> *Isaiah 41:9 (NIV)*

# HEAVEN TOGETHER

*W*e all have best friends in high school but keeping in contact through life is much less common. Most of the time it is unheard of. For me, though, it was a reality.

Trying out for the drill team in my sophomore year was probably the best thing I ever did in high school. Friendships were made not only with drill team members but band members too. We spent tons of time together in those three years. With everyday school classes, after and before school practices, summer camps, and every Friday night football half-time shows, we were very close!

Not only did I have one best friend during this time in my life, but two. My best girlfriend and I were on the drill team and my best guy friend was a drummer in the band. For our senior trip, the three of us ended up in Daytona Beach, FL. It was there that my best guy friend introduced me to my husband. Consequently, four of us became best friends! I really think that same year there was a spark between the two of them. Not ever getting together, when they both divorced, they talked even more. This raised my suspicions even higher!

Over the years, my husband and I kept in close contact with both of our buddies. When they married, had children, had good or bad situations arise or experienced deaths in their families, we were always there to see them through. One of those times was when my girlfriend found out she had breast cancer. After fighting her cancer and then going into remission, she was so encouraged! Unfortunately, it was not for long. In the summer of 2006, my friend's cancer came back with a fury. She went through another round of treatments but increasingly became worse. While she battled her cancer, our other best friend was living in another state. After not hearing from him for a few days, we were told the apartment management found his body. He tragically died at the age of 48, unexpectedly, of a heart attack!

Visiting my friend with cancer was hard enough, but having to tell her our other friend had died also, made it more difficult. We all cried together. We all knew this would be our last time to be together too. Exchanging loving words, recalling memories of old and shedding tears of sadness, my husband and I said our last good-byes.

Loosing both of our best friends wasn't easy. It still isn't! To this day, sometimes I don't want to remember they are both gone. I just want to forget it all happened! I can tell you though I know that they are happy. I will never know if my suspensions were right or not, but it no longer matters. They are together in paradise!

What about you? Will you spend eternity in Heaven? If not, don't waste a moment making your reservation. What will it hurt? I would wager to say you're better off being right at check-in time than finding out you were wrong all along if you don't!

*"The world and all its wanting, wanting, wanting is on the way out –*
*but whoever does what God wants is set for eternity."*
*1 John 2:17 (The Message)*

# THE EVIDENCE OF HER YEARS

*M*oving from my home state of Georgia to Tennessee unfortunately restricted me from being able to see family as much as I had been accustomed to. My grandmother was getting older in her years so having her and my aunt come visit periodically, along with my parents and brother, helped me settle in my new home so much easier.

When my grandmother came to visit, it helped my parents to have some much needed free time and allowed my family and me some quality time. I always tried to take care of her needs and enjoy the time we had together. Memories made would be what I lived on when she went to be with the Lord.

Upon the arrival, of one of her visits, I noticed she had a limp in her walk. Asking what was wrong, she told me her foot had been hurting for a while. Not knowing what was wrong, she just lived with her pain. Interested in what could have been the issue, I took her sock off an immediately noticed an ingrown toenail. Without hesitation, I drew a pan of hot water and soaked her painful feet. Drying them off, one by one, I carefully cleaned and cut away all of the unnecessary skin and nails from both of her feet. Amazed at the restoration of her toes, my grandmother could miraculously walk again. She was so excited. She no longer had a limp. The pedicure that transformed her indeed renewed her step!

Sitting on the floor with my grandmother's feet in hand was something I can barely describe. As I sat before her I pictured Jesus as He knelt among His disciples. I know their feet must have also included scars, dirt embedded in their skin and calluses from their walking. Although my grandmother was not a disciple, she had lived life as one. Her testimony was in her years of teaching, sharing and telling of her wisdom from her life lessons. She walked many steps while sharing incredible wisdom along the way!

What about you? Do you have a grandmother or perhaps another wise soul you seek wisdom from? Is there someone who has poured life into your walk with his or her Godly steps? Take time today to thank God for placing wise people in your life. Thank Him also for the wise ones that have invested in your life!

*"So He got up from the meal, took off His outer clothing,*
*and wrapped a towel around His waist. After that, He poured*
*water into a basin and began to wash His disciples' feet,*
*drying them with the towel that was wrapped around Him."*
*John 13:4 & 5 (NIV)*

# AN ANGEL?

During a transition in employment my brother came to live with my husband and me. Although he loved our family he was actively seeking a place to call his own.

One afternoon he had worked a little later than usual. He wasn't sure exactly when he would be off work but he always let me know. Just about dusk, I received a phone call from my brother's number. Answering it, I heard the voice of a woman on the other line I didn't know. She wanted to know if I was my brother's sister. Somewhat startled at her questioning, I ask if everything was OK. It wasn't! She went on to tell me that a car had hit my brother. Assuring me he was OK, she said the paramedics were going to transport him to the hospital. Shaken and in shock I jumped into the car speeding to the scene of the accident. I had no idea what had happened and if he really would be fine or not.

When I arrived I saw him lying in the middle of the intersection! The paramedics were checking him over and about to move him on to the stretcher. Looking around, I could not see the woman who had called me. There were only men on the scene.

Only minutes earlier my brother had entered an intersection when lumber from the back of a truck in front of him slide out into the road. Eager to help the gentleman in need, my brother pulled his car over. While the two of them were bent over picking up the wood, an elderly woman ran right through the intersection. She apparently was unable to see either of the men or the wood that had been scattered all over the road. Without warning, her car hit my brother and threw him into the air. Coming down, he landed on his leg. From his fall, he suffered a broken femur and a torn ACL and LCL. A few weeks later, he had surgery repairing all of his injuries. Fortunately, he has healed and is fine today!

Recalling the events of the accident, my brother was curious about how I had been notified of the accident. I told him I'd received a call from his phone from a woman I did not know. "*That's impossible,*" he said. "*My phone never left my pants pocket.*"

God works in mysterious ways. He charges angels to come to our aid and minister to His chosen. That day, He provided an angel for my brother and myself. He knew at that very moment I needed to be with my brother and He made a way through one of His angels!

What about you? Has God been faithful to provide an angel at any time in your life? Has He perhaps provided one you never recognized as one? Take time today to look back on your life and see where God used someone or something that you know was unexplainable. Take time to ask the Holy Spirit to reveal where He has faithfully provided an angel just in time for you!

*"Do not forget to show hospitality to strangers, for by so doing some*
*people have shown hospitality to angels without knowing it."*
*Hebrews 13:2 (NIV)*

# THE CARPORT DROP OFF

*I*n her late eighty's, my grandmother was unable to travel to church every Sunday morning. Her health forced her to redo her way of life and simply enjoy church from her living room. Television evangelism became her worship leader. Although she was unable to attend her home church, like clockwork, every Monday morning a faithful volunteer showed up in her driveway. The volunteer positioned a video copy of the past Sunday morning's sermon for my aunt and her to enjoy.

One weekend I went to my grandmother's house to visit. Meeting her in the carport, she was placing several of the VCR tapes on her freezer where the church volunteer left her weekly sermon tapes. Curious, I asked her if she had enjoyed the sermon's the church had provided. "I don't know," she replied in a soberly stoned tone. Somewhat startled at her response I said, "What do you mean you don't know?" "I haven't watched them." She said. "Well, why in the world haven't you?" I asked. "Because I don't know how to work my VCR!" she replied.

Over the course of five years, this tireless volunteer had used no telling how much gas and countless hours of time to take weekly sermon tapes to these two ladies. Because they had no idea how to run their own VCR, they just continuously repositioned the tapes every Monday morning to trade for new ones. Feeling no reason to break the volunteer's natural routine, my grandmother and aunt just continued to allow this gentlemen to provide his servant hood as he had done for many years.

As Christians, following the example of Christ causes us to mirror the image of His servant-hood. Besides His love for mankind, serving others was His ultimate goal! Many times however, Jesus was obedient to minister but some people never responded. There was no question. They saw Him. They saw what He did. But even in His obedience, the people didn't accept the gift of salvation they were offered. No matter, Jesus continued to tell the good news of the Gospel. Just like the faithful volunteer, He was tirelessly obedient and will be rewarded for His faithfulness!

What about you? Are their things in your life you are missing? Are their ones who are handing you something of value you have chosen to reject or not even view? Take time today to look around and see what you have overlooked. Take time today to reevaluate the blessings you may have missed or be the blessing to another you so obediently need to be.

> *"Jesus then left that place and went into the region of*
> *Judea and across the Jordan. Again crowds of people*
> *came to Him, and as was His custom, He taught them."*
> *Mark 10:1 (NIV)*

# THE BLOW DRYER

My dear grandmother lived the last few years of her life mentally in tack, but her bladder was another story. Everywhere she went a beach towel and plastic bag went with her. In fact, they were placed under her everywhere she sat. This routine ensured a dry seat no matter if hers wasn't. As the body ages, so does the plumbing!

One road trip to take her and my aunt home after a stay at my house, we stopped for a much needed potty break. My aunt slowly escorted my grandmother to the restroom while I unbuckled and got the children out of the car. We soon joined them inside. After the girls and I took our break and exited the stalls, I could hear some fussing going on around the corner on the other side of the restroom. Two women were going at it. As I turned the corner, I saw at the other end of the stalls, it was my own family in a squabble! Mortified, I watched as my 95 year-old grandmother was bent over with her backside in the air, nearly standing on her head. Because her pants were soiled from not making it to the potty on time, my aunt had a great idea for a remedy. She was convinced if my grandmother bent over under the hair dryer on the wall, her pants would easily dry. Consequently, they both were arguing about how long she had to stand there. My grandmother was furious that all of her blood was quickly collecting in her head. My aunt, seemingly unconcerned, just kept telling her to stand still and wait until her pants were completely dry. Continuing to bicker like two banty roosters, my children and I quickly escaped without anyone noticing we were related in any way to them!

Can you recall a time you were put in an upside down position? No matter what your position, God is there to guide you. It's often in the uncomfortable places God can change us, fix us and without redressing us, totally dry us out. He can squeeze out the ugly and dry out our insides. It's in this process that He can fill us up with Himself. Allow Him to have His way and restore you today.

*"Don't have anything to do with foolish and stupid arguments, because you know they produce quarrels. And the Lord's servant must not be quarrelsome but must be kind to everyone, able to teach, not resentful."*
*11 Timothy 2:23 & 24 (NIV)*

# In The "Nick of Time"

*E*very December, my mom and dad drive from Georgia to Nashville to have family Christmas. Christmas for our family is a time of giving. Lots of giving. Presents galore. So many presents that when they came for the holiday one particular year, the luggage had to be tied on top of the car. My aunt and grandmother were also traveling with them.

Driving up Mount Eagle, Tennessee, my mom happened to look out the side mirror. Startled, she witnessed one of the suitcases go flying off the top of the car landing in the middle of the interstate. Horrified, my dad pulled over and began backing up on the shoulder of the highway. They were determined to recover my grandmother's belongings. When my dad stopped the van and mom prepared to run to retrieve the suitcase, an 18-wheeler began his climb up the hill. Watching and hoping their fears surely wouldn't be realized, the truck showed no sign of slowing down. As the driver topped the hill, sure enough, he and his ton of weight steam rolled right over my grandmother's travel bag. Clothes and personal items exploded in a pile in the middle of the road. Mom quickly ran, retrieving all of her stuff, threw it in the car. My grandmother, seemly not interested in the fact mom had just risked her life for her, ask if she got her cigarettes in her rubble of stuff. In complete disbelief, my mother hollered NO and turned around! The rest of the trip was silent.

After finally arriving in Nashville, my grandmother decided to change clothes into her Christmas attire. As she greeted the family and walked up the bonus room steps for gift opening, we noticed something on her backside. A fresh clean mark of that 18-wheeler's tire track adorned the entire backside of her white holiday sweatshirt. Rolling with laughter, my entire family was beside themselves. My poor grandmother had no idea! At her expense, that Christmas is one we will never forget!

Are their stories you recall where you suffered an explosive, unpredictable event? Have you been the brunt of the joke or the rescuer for another? Recognize today how things, most often in life, are so unpredictable. Thank God today that He is always there to rescue us. In fact, He allowed His son to die just to save us; just in the nick of time.

> *"'Because He loves me' says the Lord, 'I will rescue him; I will protect him,*
> *for he acknowledges my name. He will call on me, and I will honor him.*
> *With long life I will satisfy him and show him my salvation."*
> *Psalm 91: 14–16 (NIV)*

# GRADUATION DAY

hat is it about the sound of the familiar notes of *Pomp and Circumstance* that makes me cry? I admit that I couldn't tell you one word of the song, if there are even any, but my eyes and heart well up with tears each and every time it's played.

Being the emotional thinker I am, when I hear this song I can't help but be reminded that another chapter in one's life is finished. I can't help but realize a brand new chapter is about to begin. Bittersweet memories of the past will be captured in our minds forever. Although the days are gone, they will be sweet reminders of people and places and times shared.

Oh Lord, how I thank You for the chance to begin anew. Anew ~ as with the glistening of the winter's first fallen snow, or the beautiful sound of a baby's first cry, or the moment when one's heart is captivated by the memory of someone who has gone before us. How good you are to us God, as you allow every moment in time to be unique to each of us.

Thank you, Lord, for all of the pomp and circumstance we are allowed to experience. Thank you God that you have created us with a memory bank to store the specialness of the days we must leave behind. May we, in the closing of our present chapters, enter our new beginnings with the freshness of Your wisdom. May we take with us precious memories that have taught us a better way. Even in the hardest of times, may we learn and apply valuable lessons as we venture into the unknown of our tomorrows! Leaning on your wisdom God, we are assured your guiding hand is certain to see us through.

Today, examine those closed doors behind you. Examine your conclusions and acknowledge the sweet things God has embedded within as they have taken root. Be encouraged, dear one, that one day we, too, will receive our final diploma, that diploma symbolizing our own accomplishments from this life. It's not too late. Take time today to let the music swell within your heart. Take time to imagine the joy of that soon-to-be glorious, Graduation Day.

*"For I know the plans I have for you, declares the Lord;*
*plans to prosper you and not to harm you;*
*plans to give you hope and a future."*
*Jeremiah 29:11 (NIV)*

# HIS PROTECTION

After two grueling days of ice-covered streets, the temperature rose enough to begin the melting process. Suffering from cabin fever, a friend and I ventured out amongst the mush. The majority of the roads had been cleared by the traffic but side roads were still an issue. Traveling on the highway was a piece of cake until a detour rerouted us on a two-lane road up a mountain stretch. Seeing the snow that still covered most of the road, needless to say, we were concerned! As we drove with caution, approaching the bend of a curve, an oversized truck could be seen in the distance. Barreling towards us at a rapid speed, it was apparent the driver was startled by the curve and the likes of another vehicle. As if in slow motion, the truck forced the wheel slinging himself back on his side of the road. No sooner had he swerved than a gigantic piece of solid ice was cast from the top of his truck. Flying through the air, I closed my eyes as I prepared for the ice to bust through my windshield. I prepared myself for the worst! In disbelief, my eyes opened to a loud crash instead that fortunately only damaged my side mirror and the hood of my car. My friend and I, with overactive beating hearts, were just fine! We were extremely thankful that God had spared our lives!

Have you ever found yourself in a moment after God's protection? Something caught your foot before it tripped the other? Something told you to look up and ahead is an oncoming car you suddenly missed? Have you ever felt the brush of angel wings and no one was around but you? How many times has something almost been disastrous and yet in a second, it was ok. How many times, under no uncertain terms, has your life been spared?

It is in these very moments that I believe God delivers us to His fatherly side. He gives us a certainty of wisdom that proves only He could have saved us. Somewhat frightened, yet secure, we do know God sends His angels to protect us.

Thank Him today for loving you enough to always have a watchful eye on you. Thank Him also for His assurance that beyond a shadow of a doubt He is certain of that which we cannot see!

*"He will command His angels concerning you, and they will lift you up in their hands, so that you will not strike your foot against a stone."*
*Matthew 4:6 (NIV)*

# GOING HOME

Facing reality isn't always easy no matter who you are! My dear friend was cancer stricken, given no hope of survival and making final preparations to say his last goodbyes. Walking with him through his journey, I was honored to be able to spend some one-on-one time with him before he passed on to be with the Lord.

Arriving at his home that Monday morning, I sat on the edge of his bed eagerly anticipating his soft-spoken words. On the verge of death, my friend shared with me what a blessing I had been to him. Somewhat shocked, I felt sure I was the one going there to tell him of the joy he had been in my life. Before his illness we began working together and he had become very dear to me. Intrigued with his wisdom of the Bible, ministry and Christianity in general, I always loved to engage in deep conversation with him. Our lives both consisted of one main goal, to worship and serve the Lord. We spent many days sharing our personal trials and triumphs and gained much needed wisdom that could be applied to our own set of circumstances.

That day, sharing the realization of his "*going home*," my friend reminded me of the sincere gratitude he possessed for my love for his children as he and his wife had. Both of his offspring had been involved in the ministry God had allowed me to serve. His thankfulness again provided confirmation of the Lord's calling on my life to become a youth minister.

It is never easy to stare death in the face. It is never easy to say one last good-bye. The very next morning, my friend took his last living breath to breathe in eternity! I am certain though that the Spirit of the living God shared those very special moments with the two of us the day before. I am also certain that even though we will never meet again on earth, my friend knows how much I respect and love him. While I was the student, he was my professor. Thankfully, he cared enough to share with me a piece of him through his wisdom.

Is there someone today you may not see tomorrow? Has God shown you someone who needs to hear your words? Maybe someone whose words you need to hear? Ask God today to reveal who He would have you visit this week. In obedience dear one, go in His name. Today may be your last opportunity.

*"Precious in the sight of the Lord is the death of His faithful servants."*
*Psalms 116:15 (NIV)*

# THE SWEETNESS OF THE PAST

There are those times in our lives that the sweet fragrance of their existence is so refreshing. Time spent with my cousins in Oklahoma is one of them. My sister and I spent time at our cousin's house every summer possible.

After twenty-two years of the inability to revisit their homestead, I planned a trip to revisit a piece of my past. My brother accompanied me to my aunt and uncle's home. We passed the lake where my sister and I once swam. We saw a neighbor's home where the two of us loved to play in the playhouse just beside the back porch. Sobered by the memories, I was even more anxious to reach our destination. Finally driving up to the familiar stop sign, we gazed over to see the house that was just as I had remembered. It was such a sweet taste to my soul. Have things changed? Absolutely. Did I remember a lot? More than I ever thought I would. As my feet guided me around the house, I stared at trinkets and furniture that seemed to captivate my memory. Those memories suddenly reactivated my childhood state. Somehow with them in mind, my sister was right there with me! The two of us danced through that property together. Hand in hand we soared to a place of freedom. We joined forces and marched over the past taking back that territory of old. We played together on the playground in the backyard. We swam over and over in the pool together. We ran the length of the property falling on the ground suddenly out of breath! We laughed at one another and played hide-and-seek until dark. We sat on the front lawn at night and watched the fireflies light up the sky. We lived as playmates and best friends in the presence of our favorite cousins! We were somehow together once again!

Today, life indeed is different. My sister lives no more. Yesterday is surely gone. No matter though, the sweet unchangeable memories will live within forever! I will treasure that past with her in my memories.

Are there places you need to perhaps revisit? Maybe you need to simply walk on a quiet road or fly across the skies. Have the Savior travel with you. Allow Him to guide you back in time. Experience with Him the fragrance of the sweetness of your past.

*"For everything that was written in the past was written to teach us,*
*so that through the endurance taught in the Scriptures and*
*the encouragement they provide we might have hope."*
*Romans 15:4 (NIV)*

# LITTLE UNDERSTANDING

*B*eing a youth minister allowed me to come in contact with many incredible youth. As time went on, the Lord brought them full circle to celebrate marriages, births and other accomplishments in their lives. The one thing I never wanted to experience was death. Unfortunately, sometimes we must.

I had not seen this young woman in a few years. Her mother and I kept up and she always updated me on her daughter. The phone call I got this particular morning was not one I ever expected to get. The young woman I had ministered to was on the way to the hospital. Her baby was five and a half weeks and not breathing. Immediately praying, I waited for an update. Unfortunately, the update was not good news. Her sweet baby girl had gone to be with the Lord.

Completely hysterical, she asked me to come to their home. I was at a loss for words. I had never experienced anything like this. I was assured though that the Holy Spirit had the exact words these two young people needed.

The day of her funeral was a very grueling day for the family. Questions unanswered, their future unpredictable and life now standing still. Their daughter was the most gorgeous child I had ever seen. She looked just like an angel in her long white gown. Beauty adorned her.

After the service, the family continued to the graveside for her burial. It was a beautiful fall day. The weather was comfortable outside. Lined in their chairs, the family listened as a scripture was read and a prayer prayed. Once the ceremony was concluded, her sweet baby's casket was lowered into the ground. No one moved. The silence was piercing. Standing beside the tent, I noticed a tree next to me. Looking up, in the top of the tree, was a little bird that had flown to watch the ceremony. The bird never made a sound. His body perched in a stilled position; he kept his eyes affixed on the dirt that was being scooped into the hole. Watching the bird and hearing the sound of every move the shovel made, he remained frozen. Finally, at the last pat of dirt and flowers placed on the grave, the bird miraculously flew away. Never making a sound, he just flew away.

I wonder to this day what that bird symbolized. His unmistakable reverence for the burial was incredible to me. I do believe, however, even the Lord has a way of allowing us to see His majesty even in the midst of pain and sorrow. This day was no exception.

How has God's majesty shown in the midst of your pain? Has He come to your aid? Take time today to thank Him for never leaving you. Thank Him for always being your strength and guide in the weakest, most unpredictable times of your life. Thank Him today for being God of all!

*"But He said to me, 'My grace is sufficient for you, for my power is made*
*perfect in weakness.' Therefore I will boast all the more gladly about*
*my weaknesses, so that Christ's power may rest on me."*
*11 Corinthians 12:9 (NIV)*

# THE GIFT OF YOU

*A*dmiring her family portraits, I gently placed them back on top of the stacks of books that lined her shelves. The dusting was complete and I knew my rearranging of her nick nacks would please her worn out body even more. This particular day, God allowed a friend and me to clean house for a very special person. Tired from the strain of chemotherapy, she gratefully accepted our invitation to help get her house back in order. Making sure each room was straightened and cleaned to her perfection, she was able to rest much easier. Every woman's home is her castle!

After getting everything in order, the three of us sat together and just enjoyed one another's company. It was such a sweet time of reflection. We recalled the closeness we had once shared from days gone by. In the few hours we were together we rejoiced in the Lord for allowing our paths to cross. We laughed, we talked and we recalled so many stories from days gone by. We remembered how fortunate we were to have shared so many special times together. In the presence of God, we thanked Him for our friendships!

Finally, knowing we had to get back to our families, the three of us sat holding hands in the middle of her living room. With tears of joy we thanked God for our precious moments together that day. We thanked Him for the opportunity He gave us to serve our precious sister in her time of need. We were blessed, even in the unfortunate circumstance of her illness. God faithfully used that time for good. Together again, we made the best of it. We renewed our friendships and were so very thankful for the moments we would cherish for a lifetime.

I was again reminded that there is no better feeling than the giving of myself to someone in need. Oh what joy it is to allow one's self to be a helpmate especially among friends. We may not always know what others are facing, but somehow the Spirit will always clue us in.

When was the last time you gave the gift of you? When was God able to steer your path to spend time with another in need? Allow Him to speak today. Allow Him to use you in a miraculous and encouraging way.

*"You will be enriched in every way so that you can be generous on every occasion,*
*and through us your generosity will result in thanksgiving to God."*
*11 Corinthians 9:11 (NIV)*

# THE LEADING ROLE

*T*here were six of us. We spent almost every weekend together as best friends often do. One particular weekend we made plans to have dinner and see a movie. The movie was the new release of Nicholas Sparks, "*The Notebook.*"

Although the movie was romantic and clearly a "girlie flick," our spouses agreed to allow us the pleasure of their company. (Sappy movies were surely not the norm for our manly men!) With an excellent cast, however, we were all convinced it would be an incredible watch!

The film was amazing from start to finish. Dazzled by the actors' intensive portrayal of unmistakable love for one another, we were all challenged. It seemed each of us were reminded of the passion of love we also possessed for our own seasoned mate.

Ending with an unexpected conclusion, nearly every individual in the theatre was moved. In fact, so moved that almost all of us were choking, holding back our whaling and tears. Everyone except my husband that is! Yes, all five of us, along with the rest of the viewers, just sat still in our seats. For an extra few minutes we simply soaked up the reality of the two lives we had just witnessed live and die on the screen. My husband, however, stood up, looked at our sobbing beings and *unemotionally* walked right out of the theatre. After catching our breaths and coming back to reality, the five of us met him in the lobby.

Isn't that how we all can be sometimes? When the best things in life are staring us in the face, we refuse to even acknowledge them, much less respond to or be affected by them.

Life comes but only once. With ups and downs and good and bad, we have to face the reality of our role. We can't ignore the pain, the suffering, the unpleasant or the uncomfortable. We have to walk life out and decide if we will live life to the fullest, as God stands with us, or allow life to totally pass us by!

Where are you today in the grand scheme of things? Are you overwhelmed and reacting to your reality or pretending it's not reality at all? God is in the acting business. If we let Him, He acts on our behalf. Leading, guiding, directing and walking beside us, He is there every step of the way. The question is will you allow Him? Will you allow Him the lead role in the story of your life?

*"A time to weep, and a time to laugh; a time to mourn, and a time to dance; a time to cast away stones, and a time to gather stones together; a time to embrace, and a time to refrain from embracing; a time to seek, and a time to lose; a time to keep, and a time to cast away;"*
*Ecclesiastes 3:4-6 (ESV)*

# A MATTER OF LIFE AND DEATH

*I*t was a cold week in February in Mayfield, New York. My brother-in-law and niece were living there. Moving from Georgia, after my sister passed away, they had just celebrated ten years of living there. Loosing her mother at the age of two, my niece was now twelve.

At the beginning of the week, my brother-in-law suffered from some serious chest pains. Going to the Emergency Room, the doctor suggested he be hospitalized immediately. My brother-in-law wasn't well and the doctor was afraid he was on the verge of a heart attack. He politely thanked the staff but refused to stay. His daughter was number one in his life and there was no one to keep her. She had school so he told them he would just come back on the weekend. Releasing himself, without the recommendation of the doctor, my brother-in-law filled his prescription for his nitro-glycerin tablets and left the hospital.

On the way home, he explained to his daughter about the pills he had to take in case he had chest pains again. He told her where he kept them and how to administer them if he needed her too. He also told her not to worry. He would be fine.

Unfortunately, he was not fine. Not fine at all! On Saturday morning of that same week, he began having chest pains again. Screaming at his daughter to dial 911, she dialed his cell phone and ran outside to his jeep to retrieve his pills. When she got back in the house, he was unconscious. She administered the tablet as instructed and stayed on the phone with 911. With an ambulance finally arriving, they took my brother-in-law to the closest hospital. He was pronounced dead on arrival. The unfortunate thing was my niece had no idea he was gone. Getting to the hospital, the doctor told her that her daddy didn't make it. She had now lost both of her parents!

A few of my family members and I immediately flew to New York to be with her and his family. In the course of our stay, The North Hampton Ambulance Service in Hampton, New York honored my niece. Her award was a *"Certificate of Valor"* for her *"courage and bravery when faced with an emergency."* Her call to 911 on her dad's behalf earned her this honor. As well as the recipient of the award, she was taken on a tour of the emergency area where her call was received. Although her daddy was gone, she would always know she was a true hero!

Life isn't always easy. Facing emergency situations and living out harsh unexpected realities aren't easy things. They are in fact some of the most difficult events we face in our lives. Although the realities we often face are unpredictable, God isn't. Promising to be our comforter, bind up our wounds, and restore our broken hearts, we can always count on Him. Healing our hurts is His specialty. Taking care of us is His plan as our Father. What does God need to do for you? Are there fresh wounds you need healed? Perhaps there are old scars that just keep tearing open. Take time today to go to your Father for restoration. Go to Him trusting He will do as He says; to make you new again!

*"And I will ask the Father, and He will give you another*
*Advocate to help you and be with you forever."*
*John14:16 (NIV)*

# THE UNIMAGINABLE

*M*y college roommate and I are best friends. In fact, to this day we call each other "bestest friends at Reinhardt or short, BFAR." We graduated from Reinhardt College together in 1979 and have continued to be dear friends throughout the years. We attended one another's weddings, experienced the births of each other's babies, and even comforted the other when our close family members passed away. It is just understood that we will always be there for the other!

One tragic memory I won't ever forget was the unexpected death of her teenage son. When she called me that afternoon from Georgia, I immediately left Tennessee to be by her side. There was no question in my mind that I had to be with her. I knew her heart was shattered in a million pieces!

With strength like no one I'd ever seen, she sat amongst a sea of mourners at the funeral home and greeted each individual in line. For hours she sat and greeted. From birth until death, she expressed her gratitude to those who had been a part of her baby son's eighteen years of life. She talked to many that just shared their condolences and others; she listened and clung onto every word they spoke. There were stories she had never heard. There were stories she wanted to hear again and again. Without question, the face of each person there that evening created a beautiful melody of her son's existence on earth.

Our distance from state to state did not allow me to know her precious boy. In the company of those who did, however, I was able to see a glimpse of this precious young man. The kind words, the funny stories, and the personality traits of his wonderful mom made it obvious that he was a joy to know and love.

Unlike most, my friend knows firsthand the sacrifice of flesh of her flesh, bone of her bone, and the core of her being. (I am reminded of our Heavenly Father, who just like my friend, knows firsthand the pain of the sacrifice of a precious son.) I am thankful though, that we serve a God who promises to be a comforter in our place of hurt and broken heartedness.

Are there unexpected and painful sacrifices you, too, have made in life? Is there a loved one that you long to embrace again in eternity? Take your sorrow to the Father today. He knows all about your pain and suffering! He knows all too well the ache within your heart and is experienced in soothing your pain. He would love more than anything to bind up your broken heart today!

*"For God so loved the world that He gave His only begotten Son, that*
*whosoever believeth in Him should not perish but have everlasting life."*
*John 3:16 (KJV)*

# THE WORN OUT RAGS

*I* watched from a distance as my 90-year-old grandmother sat for hours at my kitchen table. With scissors in hand, she carefully cut every strand of thread that hung from my 24 year old towels. Intrigued by her diligence, I watched as she precisely cut and created each one to look as if it were new again. Once the strands were removed by the skill of her hands, she placed each one on the table and carefully ironed and folded and ironed and folded until they looked as good as new again! Although the many years of washing had loosened the threads and wrinkled the material she could envision the recreation of a perfectly good worn out rag.

My life has been like that of those towels. The longer I live, the more worn out I become. I've listened and been obedient. I've listened and not done what was right. Doing things my way has often cost me. I have seen the good from my actions and I have felt the bad. I have lived many years with the consequences of my mistakes and I've reaped the blessings from my obedience. Like those towels, though, my mistakes have caused the pulling of the threads from my fabric. I have been loosened from all ends. I have suffered from my decisions and at times it has wrinkled my appearance. Life is hard! Although I know I must learn from my mistakes, God's Word wants to save me the trouble. Obedience is the best way but there is still hope if we insist on doing things our way!

With dangling threads and wrinkles alike, God still sees us through His eyes. He sees us new! When we finally sit before Him in obedience, He will cut away our worn out strands. He alone can press out the wrinkles and fashion us in a whole new way. Until we allow Him the ability to straighten out and prune the dead in us, we will remain tattered and worn, never looking or being our very best! More than anything's He wants to mold us into the person He has intended us to be!

Thank God today for pruning your dangling strands that bind. Thank Him today for His diligence in creating that perfect masterpiece He created you to be.

*"Create in me a pure heart, Oh God, and renew a steadfast spirit within me.*
*Do not cast me from your presence, or take your Holy Spirit from me. Restore*
*to me the joy of your salvation and grant me a willing spirit, to sustain me."*
*Psalm 51:10-12 (NIV)*

# HOLIDAY DECORATING

*D*ecorating for Christmas at my house is not a simple task. In fact, it requires weeks' worth of hard work to complete! Bringing boxes down from the attic is just one of the necessities in preparation not to mention the rearrangement of everything in my entire house!

Thirty-six years of marriage has increased the number of ornaments for our family tree and house decorations. Every Christmas our kids were creating their own adornments and trinkets at school, some were received as gifts from special friends and, of course, I have personally always donated while Christmas shopping! Our 'load' has grown so much over the years that we've required more and more and more boxes to store our holiday treasures!

One year in particular, while unpacking my boxes, I was silently reminded of how thankful I am for my mom. Precisely placing each figurine in the nativity scene, I watched my mother decorate with her special touch. Over the years, I have collected visions of her skills, the warmth of her magical handiwork, and the wisdom of her ways. Together, I have molded my own skills with her motherly decorating touch. Waiting in anticipation every year to see the finished product of her decorating skills inspired me every time! I can hardly wait to begin the process each and every year!

I am so thankful for the traditions of our family. I trust that my offspring will as well grasp a hold of the beauty of our history while they add their special uniqueness. From Christmas dishes to an artificial tree, from fresh cut cedar branches, to that special nativity scene, from decorated tables, to framed family portraits by the tree, I am so very grateful! I hold all of my own memories, which I replay year after year. No matter what each season may bring, the heart of the holiday is captured in memories of the past. The skills are gifts from the ones who have taught us how to truly celebrate.

What about you? Has God blessed you with a mom that handed you a piece of your family heritage through tradition? Do you have the opportunity to share your own traditions with your own children? Thank God today for the gift of family. Thank Him, too, that you are a necessary link in the tradition to pass on something special to your own precious children.

> *"By wisdom a house is built, and through understanding it is established;*
> *through knowledge its rooms are filled with rare and beautiful treasures."*
> *Proverbs 24:3&4 (NIV)*

# RESTORING MY LOSS

*J*n the fall of 1996, God placed a calling on my life to minister to youth. Having a teenage son, I believe, created a prime opportunity for me to become involved.

After two and a half years of serving, the ministry I was involved in took a turn in a different direction. I wasn't prepared for the turn nor did I expect it. Consequently, I resigned my position with the youth.

The loss of the youth group that I had groomed and nurtured wasn't easy. In fact, it took a huge toll on me emotionally. Although I knew I had been obedient in my decision, it was still painful. Very painful! Eventually though, I did heal. God used that experience to groom me specifically for the future assignments on my ministry journey. Showing me a vision was proof of the healing He had done in my life, healing from the inside out.

The vision was of a once beautiful farmhouse. (Even as a little girl, I always wanted to live in one.) This homestead, however, was unique to me. It symbolized the ministry I lost. The house was not standing anymore. It had completely burned down. All I could see was the remains of what used to be life within the walls. When I looked at the concrete foundation, all that was visible was a sea of ashes. The ashes represented the death of what once had been. Glancing over the rubble, I saw a shimmering light in the midst of all the ashes. Stepping into the remains, I reached down and began combing through the ashes. Amazed at the beauty, I uncovered a huge shinny diamond. The diamond was radiant. It was the heat from the fire that made the diamond shine.

Although the homestead represented the past that I had lost, the future was shown to me in the beauty of the diamond. Restoration comes when we are willing to gain wisdom from our experiences and then use them to minister to others. God was not only restoring me, but my testimony and my ministry! What a faithful God we serve!

What is it today that God wants to restore in your life? Have you suffered a loss He can refine? Have you given up something that has broken your heart? Allow your Heavenly Father to begin a new work in you. Allow Him to have complete control and turn your ashes into beauty the way only God can do!

*"The Spirit of the Sovereign Lord is on me, because the Lord has anointed me to proclaim good news to the poor. He has sent me to bind up the brokenhearted, to proclaim freedom for the captives and release from darkness for the prisoners, to proclaim the year of the Lord's favor and the day of vengeance of our God, to comfort all who mourn, and provide for those who grieve in Zion—to bestow on them a crown of beauty instead of ashes, the oil of joy instead of mourning, and a garment of praise instead of a spirit of despair."*
*Isaiah 61:1-3 (NIV)*

# My Other House

*A*dmitting your shortcomings are not easy to do. Feelings and affects of failure or the reality of criticism are also extremely hard to endure. I know this first hand! One of my biggest shortcomings was my addiction to cigarettes.

Although I quit for a couple of years, I picked up the nasty habit again. Living in a town where smokers were looked down upon, I hid my addiction as best I could. Since I had received a call on my life to minister to youth, my biggest fear was being 'found out'. No doubt it certainly would taint opinions of me as an example to teens. I decided to satisfy my strong desire to smoke; hiding my habit was my only option. For a while, I was even able to keep the secret from my own children.

Our house had a seven-foot crawl space. Although poorly lit with a dirt floor, it was an excellent place to store things. Complete with our patio furniture and an ashtray, it became my official 'smoke hole'. Hiding under there was the perfect set up! Throughout the day, I'd sneak in my 'hole' and smoke away. Coming up with excuse after excuse to keep everyone from finding me, I continued my pattern. Complete with vent peep holes; I could see if anyone came to my house. It gave me time to run out and get back upstairs before being caught. Even my other smoke buddy girlfriends would join me there. It got to be a ridiculous joke renaming my space my "other house!"

After much conviction and prayers I finally gave up my habit. Coming clean allowed me to come out of the basement and back into the light of my real home. Although it was a daily walk for a while eventually my desire to smoke was gone. No longer was I compelled to sneak, hide, lie or pretend I was something I wasn't. How grateful I am today that I don't have to worry about what others say or live with the agony of keeping my secret.

Often times in life, we are faced with issues that weigh us down. We allow things to become so attached to us that we can't even breathe. In fact, the breath is nearly sucked out of us. Thankfully, God is our life preserver. Becoming the weightlessness needed to keep us afloat, He safely takes us to shore. And in the process, we are able to recharge, regenerate and reposition our state of mind. In doing so, we see where the enemy tried so desperately to drown us. We see, with his help, how we nearly killed ourselves!

What about you? Are there pressures, addictions or attractions that have you bound? Is the breath almost sucked out of you? Take time today to evaluate the real issues you face. Take time today to allow the Holy Spirit to recharge and redo the things only He can do. Allow Him to mold you into the prize possession you are to Him!

*"Truly I tell you, whatever you bind on earth will be bound in Heaven, and whatever you loose on earth will be loosed in Heaven."*
*Matthew 18:18 (NIV)*

# In His Hands

*I*t was a fall morning and I was getting ready for work. My husband was on the road. As usual, I was anxiously awaiting his return home the next day.

While putting on my make-up, I turned on the local news. The broadcast was suddenly interrupted. It was a *Special News Report* from Washington. Terrorists had hijacked four commercial passenger jet airliners. Two of the planes had crashed into the Twin Towers of the World Trade Center in New York City. A third plane went down on The Pentagon in Arlington, Virginia. The fourth plane had crashed in a field in Shanksville in rural Pennsylvania. The hijackers had redirected the flight to target either the Capitol Building or the White House. There were no survivors on any of the flights. It was believed that these incidents were terrorist attacks on the United States by al-Qaeda.

Completely sobered by the news, I suddenly remembered my husband was due to fly out of Washington D.C. this very day at 8:15 a.m. from the same airport as the hijackings. Contacting his office, his secretary confirmed his flight and let me know she had not been able to reach him. At this point, I had no idea where he was. He was in the air or perhaps on one of the planes that had crashed? I was horrified!

Finally a few hours later, he called. Since he had been in the air, he was completely unaware of what had just occurred in our country. Getting into the airport, he realized the terror America was facing. He also discovered the President of the United States' private plane had just landed at the same airport he had landed. This instantly made his location another target. Finally he was able to begin his journey back home.

Due to this tragic misfortune, for the first time in history, all planes in the air were instructed by the FAA to land at the nearest airport and the airways were completely cleared. On the evening of September 11, 2001, the American sky was completely dark. Only the moon and stars lit the night. Sitting on my deck as my mind recaptured the day's events, I felt extremely thankful for my husband's survival. I will never forget the silence or the darkness that penetrated that unforgettable evening's sky.

Our world has not been promised a Cinderella story. In fact, quite the opposite. Satan and his demons will continue to prowl around this earth until his final day of torture. In the midst of all the terror, God is faithful to His chosen people. He promises to guide and protect those that choose to obey and believe in Him.

What about you? Have you chosen to follow the light or rest in the darkness? Have you given your life for Christ to use as an example to a lost and fallen world or chosen to be caught up in the wickedness of the present day enemy? Take time today to evaluate your fate. Take time to know where you will spend eternity.

*"And the devil, who deceived them, was thrown into the lake of*
*burning sulfur, where the beast and the false prophet had been*
*thrown. They will be tormented day and night for ever and ever."*
*Revelation 20:10 (NIV)*

# TURBO POWER!

When I sleep, I always love listening to the sound of a fan. In high school, my family lived in a two-story home that was equipped with an amazing attic fan. Our fan generated air throughout the house when the windows were open. There was absolutely nothing quiet about it either. When you turned it on, the roar was like that of a lion, resonating throughout the house. On hot summer evenings, the air breezing through was so relaxing and strangely enough, tranquilizing.

My love for the sound began as an infant. When my parents lived in their small one bedroom apartment, it was extremely hot in the summer. Not being able to afford air conditioning made way for a permanent box fan. It ran continuously and soothed me to sleep every night. All of my life, that fan was my sedative for slumber!

As an adult, I have to admit, I am still hypnotized by the sound. I can sleep like a baby anytime of the day when it is cranked up. As I've gotten older though, I will say it has become even harder to fall asleep. I think that's part of the "*growing older*" package. My box fan is a permanent fixture now. I don't leave home without it and I can't sleep without it. The sad part is, because of my addiction to that fan, two of my three children own and use one too!

God wants to be that permanent fixture in our life also. He wants us to carry Him wherever we go. He wants us to depend on Him to take care of the restlessness we face in the various situations in our lives. It's in the allowing of Him to transform our inability to face certain circumstances that we are able to find tranquility in situations.

Where is it that you have placed God in your life? Have you chosen to take Him wherever you go, whenever you go? Do you pick and choose where He is in your daily walk? Take time today to evaluate where God fits in in your life. Take time to see where He needs to be put back where He has been taken out or possibly never allowed. Realize today that God wants all of you in every area of who you are.

*"One thing I ask of the Lord, this is what I seek: that I may dwell in the house of the Lord all the days of my life, to gaze on the beauty of the Lord and to seek Him in His temple."*
*Psalm 27:4 (NIV)*

# In His Breath

*I* am the night owl in my family. It has always been this way and to be honest, I like it. Like the sound of the violent wind on that day of Pentecost, I'd get my children to bed my body would be transformed. Suddenly, the inflammation of productivity would captivate my being. Now, mind you, I consider myself a simple person. Somehow, though, this brain of mine had to be exercised. Writing a poem, reading a book or penning encouraging scribbles to a friend, I'd stay up like a cat lurking for his prey. Night after night, I'd look so forward to the salvation of those hours alone.

After all these years, probably from the age of 16, God has continually invaded my brain. With pen or computer in hand, He'd use this vessel as His own creative writing tool. Over and over, season after season, I'd dash for the first instrument that was saturated with ink. The closest piece of paper, like the deposit slip with my lip prints all over it, was yanked as a pad. Cautiously and creatively, the Lord dictated the lesson. Word after word rushed to my thinking. I know this effort was not of my own creation. It was clearly obvious by the shocking reaction I'd always have. Each time I would be amazed at the masterpiece of His completed product.

Over and over, time and again, God has been faithful. Somehow, someway, the He in me has produced the one He wants others to see. In letters of encouragement or devotions on a page, the best of God is filtered through the imperfections in me. Do I deserve it? No! Do I take credit for it? Yea a little maybe. All I know is God in His mightiness has something to give us all. Exhibited through taking our vocal chords and strumming them aloud, or running one's legs out on the court, God has a gift He instills within us. Today, I finally call myself a writer. The best, hardly. Chosen? Yes, that's me. For God in His awesomeness knows my name. He is the One who has created this me.

What is it today, God has released in you? What talent is it your Father has placed deep inside? Take time today to reflect on the work He's doing beneath. Take time to bathe in the breath He has so preciously breathed into you!

*"We have different gifts, according to the grace given to each of us."*
*Romans 12:6 (NIV)*

# MEMORIES IN MY NOTES

*L*iving in Nashville, Tennessee allowed me the opportunity to meet one of my best friends. We were very much alike. As the years went on, our relationship deepened. Our friendship turned into sisterhood.

After 25 years of marriage, my best friend and her husband agreed to divorce. It was a situation where my dear friend had to move from Nashville to Oklahoma. It was too many miles away for me but there was nothing I could do to keep her here. Knowing the emotional strain she and her soon-to-be ex-husband had already been through I volunteered to help them pack.

While the two of them talked out their differences and prepared for their departure, I packed their belongings. I divided 25 years of things they once shared. From dishes to spices, everything was halved. While packing her boxes, I couldn't help but be reminded of the numerous memories our families had shared with one another. As I began to pack up her items, I grabbed a pack of sticky notes. For every box I packed, I included a note that shared a memory of our times together. The box with her recipe books included a reminder note of my favorite dishes that she had cooked for me. The box that held the pictures of the family vacations we shared contained a note recalling a special memory from our trips. The box that held her Christian books and devotionals had a note that recalled the many times we shared words of encouragement from God's perspective.

Each box had it's own special remembrance of our past. The stories and moments in time were recorded like a history lesson. It was not until she reached her new home and began unpacking each box that she found each note. Although we were miles apart, a piece of me was with her in my handwritten remembrances.

God, too, shares in our remembering. He reminds us of the many times He has stood and fought our fights. He recaptures the moments He has bore our sorrows. He has never left us or forsaken us. He has always walked beside us every step we've taken. In joy and in sorrow, He has been there. In good times and bad, He was present.

What is it today God has walked you through? What is it that your Heavenly Father needs to remind you of even if it hurts? Take time to reflect on His provision. Take time to recognize His care. Let Him know just how grateful you are for His constant love and affection for all His children.

*"'He will cover you with His feathers, and under His wings you will find refuge;*
*His faithfulness will be your shield and rampart.'"*
*Psalm 91:14 (NIV)*

# THE ROUND ABOUT

There were four of us. We were the best of friends. Unfortunately, life and all of its changes changed us. All three of them were drawn away from our little town from job transfers to new ventures in life. Promising to continue our friendship the best we could, we planned a weekend retreat in Tampa, FL.

We had such a great trip! We spent time catching up in conversation, laughter, sun bathing and just being together again.

After dinner one evening, we drove to the middle of town. We had plans of venturing out beyond the norm. (Actually, after our normal 9:00 p.m. bedtimes.) The funny thing was, directly in the center of town, the four oncoming roads joined forces to make a circular path. That path literally went round and round. I'd never seen or heard of anything like it. (They called it a "round about"!) While the two were gabbing in the backseat catching up, the two of us in the front seat had a grand idea. Grinning at one another at the exact same time, the driver just kept driving around and around that "round about." Laughing uncontrollably, as my friends continued to gab, we wondered just how long it would take them to realize we were going in a continuous circle. Sure enough, after hearing our chuckles and feeling the effects of the dizziness coming on, our friends realized the continuous circle we were making.

Oh how fun it is to laugh; how fun it is to be on the merry-go-round of life. Sometimes, though, if we don't pay close attention to our drive, we will lose track of time and the dizziness can quickly set in. We can wonder off track if we aren't careful. Although "laughter is good for the soul," it's always good to know when to stop. We need to know when to stop, get off the circle and move on down the road of life.

What about you? Have you found yourself going round and round in circles? Is your path really not going anywhere in particular? Take time today to examine your road.

Take time to see if you have stopped for a much needed laugh or two. Are your circles overwhelming you, or honestly, simply getting the best of you? Ask God today to slow you down. Ask Him to help you balance the circles and the laughter in your life.

*"Our mouths were filled with laughter, our tongues with songs of joy. Then it*
*was said among the nations, The Lord has done great things for them.*
*The Lord has done great things for us, and we are filled with joy."*
*Psalm 126: 2 & 3 (NIV)*

# FAMILY TREE

One evening, my baby boy lay sleeping, cradled in my arms. His dad and I just couldn't take our eyes off the miracle God had created. We were both so thankful for his precious little life. Our hearts were so filled with joy that our emotions promoted a wave of tears of thanksgiving within both of us!

We were so proud of our son but strangely bothered with the idea of how we could ever share our love with another child. Trusting God, though, He placed in us the desire to grow our family even more. His plan included more children in our lives!

Trying for nearly two years to conceive, we were unsuccessful. Month after month, the results were negative. I couldn't understand why God had placed this desire in us only to not allow the blessing of another pregnancy. Finally after much disappointment, I went to the doctor to be checked. I wanted to make sure all was OK even though I had already birthed one baby. With a clean bill of health, my doctor prescribed fertility medication to enhance the process. Again, month after month, the results remained negative! The doctor was as puzzled as we were at this point because there was no medical reason I was not pregnant. Finally after months of being unsuccessful, I decided to change things. I threw away the medication I had been advised to take and turned it all over to God. The heart wrenching pain of not getting pregnant had taken a toll on both of us!

It was four months after relying solely on God that I finally conceived our second child. Knowing that physically there was no reason we could not become pregnant, I then realized God had previously intentionally closed my womb. He was in control of the timing of her birth! He was the one with the plan!

Exactly five years later, our first little girl was born, and again five years later another joined our family's nest. God in His glory placed the exact amount of time between our children as He had done between my husband and his brothers. As we began to calculate, we realized something even more amazing. There was eleven years between our oldest and our youngest as there was between both my brother and I and my husband's brother and him. Three generations of eleven years apart. Indeed God's plan was to time the birth of our children as His predestined 'tradition' would have it. In His direction, He was the ultimate dictator of our family tree.

What is it today you are trying to control? What is it you need to let God plan? Take heed my friend. God will answer at just the right times: in only His precious time.

*"I prayed for this child, and the Lord has granted me what I*
*asked of Him. So now I give him to the Lord."*
*1 Samuel 1:27 & 28a (NIV)*

# I WOULD HAVE NEVER GUESSED

*I*t was our twenty-fifth wedding anniversary. We booked a cruise with two other couples to celebrate. We were going to visit the Bahamas, St. Thomas, and Puerto Rico. The day before our departure, my husband booked tickets to see Martina McBride along with back stage passes. Any other week, I would have been so excited. This week I wasn't. Not only had I not packed for our trip the next morning but my parents, grandmother and aunt had all come to spend the weekend with us. The plan was for them to stay with the children while we went on our cruise.

Although Martina was one of my very favorite singers, I was very unhappy about having to stop, get dressed up, and loose valuable time going to this concert. My husband not only would not budge on canceling his plan but completely ignored my complaints! That irritated me more! I was mad! I didn't want to go but I was being forced to go. Finally arriving at our friends' home, my two girlfriends whisked me up and pulled me up the back steps into one of the bedrooms to show me something. I was sure what was going on. They had never acted so strangely! Peering over into her grandson's baby bed was a beautiful bouquet of flowers. My girlfriend picked them up, handed them to me and then nearly pushed me down her living room staircase. I was completely caught off guard and not sure at this point what was happening. As I looked down at the bottom of the stairs, immediately I saw another friend sitting at his piano. He was playing such beautiful music. I stood for a second trying to comprehend the moment when I recognized the tune. It was the wedding march. Walking down the stairs, I finally got a glimpse of several of my other friends and family gathered in their living room. Getting closer, I could see my husband and children lined up at the fireplace looking up at me with huge grins on their faces. It was at a wedding. I was the bride and it was my wedding! My sweet husband and friends had planned a renewal of our vows honoring our twenty-five years of marriage. Needless to say, I was in complete shock! Finally reaching the front of the room, my husband and I, in the midst of our grown children, family and friends, renewed our vows.

I began feeling guilty of my behavior when I realized there was no concert! That was a setup to keep from spoiling my husband's surprise! It was a wonderful night after all. It was a night our family will never forget! It was a night recorded in our very own history book!

God has moments that have gone down in His history book as well. In His Word He promises if we call upon and believe in Him, He will renew us, restore us and remake us into His image. No matter how long it takes, He will be there when we give our all to the one who gave His all for us.

What about you? Have you given your life to Christ? Have you realized that life will never be complete without Him? Take time today to grasp that you are His own. If not, don't waste another moment. Give Him your all today!

*"For you granted Him authority over all people that He might*
*give eternal life to all those you have given Him."*
*John 17:2 (NIV)*

# A SMALL PEA

*A*fter many years of needing to clean my grandmother's home, my mother asked me to make a trip to Georgia to help. Glad to, I made arrangements to stay the week. Every day was busy. Going through 95 years of my grandmother's collection of things took time.

With each passing day, however, I often had to take a break to lie down. I was experiencing intense stomach pains and nausea. With a prior diagnosis of acid reflux, I contributed my symptoms to that. Finally, on the last day of my stay the pains became more severe. I was unable to endure them any longer so I went to the Emergency Room.

After admitting me, the doctor administered medication to try and relieve my intense pain. By this time, my mother, daughter, and cousin had joined me in the exam room. In just a few minutes, I began to break out with a rash. Allergic to the painkiller, a nurse was called. Benadryl was then administered to stop the itching and rash. The syringe the nurse used was huge. In fact, to this day, I am convinced she administered way too much medication! Fortunately, it was injected into my IV. At least I thought so. As soon as the injection was made, I felt faint. Sitting up in the bed, I immediately went limp. I had just enough strength to say, " I'm going to pass out." Sure enough, I did. Minutes later, I could hear the commotion in my room. I could hear the doctor calling my name. The bad part was I couldn't respond. My body would not respond. Feeling as if I were a small pea inside of my body, I knew I had to muster up enough energy to open my eyes. If I did not, I was afraid they would think I was dead. Talking myself into it, I finally opened them with every bit of energy I possessed. Coming to, I was quickly moved to ICU for a week where I was diagnosed with Pancreatitis. Recovery was slow after gallstone and gall bladder surgery two weeks later but I was finally on the way to feeling normal again.

We never know what can be happening inside our bodies. Signs may appear but sometimes we are misdiagnosed and the problem remains until we can get to the core of the problem. It's in the understanding we can adequately be repaired. Our life is the same way. God is the mighty physician. He is ready and available to administer the perfect cure for any of our needs. If we allow Him access to our secret places, the cure is inevitable.

What about you? Are you feeling faint? Are you diseased? Are you in a state of needing a real diagnosing? Take time today to go to the Father. Take time to allow Him to give you the cure for what you need in your life. Give Him full rein to perform a miracle that just might save your very life!

*"But I will restore you to health and heal your wounds, declares the Lord."*
*Jeremiah 30:17 (NIV)*

# AN INCREDIBLE BIRTHDAY GIFT

*M*y daughter-in-law is one of the most creative woman I know. She designs birthday cakes, birthday cards, creative poetry and always delivers the cleverest gifts! On my forty-ninth birthday, she came up with one I will never forget! Sitting in my bonus room I opened my homemade birthday card from her and my son. There was a poem etched on the inside of it. Reading it silently, I suddenly screamed. With my eyes filled with tears, it was verified that I would officially be a grandmother for the first time! I was so very excited!

Sure enough, in the early morning of June 27, 2008, my daughter-in-law's water broke. They were off to the hospital to have our new grandbaby! We already knew from the sonograms that he was a baby boy. His name was Cade Alan.

The day was filled with anticipation and eagerness as we all waited for baby Cade's arrival. Great grandparents, grandparents, parents, sisters, brothers, in-laws, friends and other family members were all there for the big moment. Unable to birth him naturally, my grandson's mommy was taken to the operating room for a cesarean section. Finally at 8:00 p.m. she delivered our first grandson. He weighed 8 pounds and was 20 inches long.

I will never forget standing in the hallway of the nursery waiting for the elevator door to open because when it opened we knew our son would be holding his new son. His firstborn son! Eyes affixed, the doors opened and with tears in his eyes, my son walked his precious baby over for the family to meet. He was beautiful! He was a miracle! He had a head full of brown hair and looked so much like our baby boy when he was born. With hearts overflowing with indescribable joy, it was one of the most wonderful days of our lives. Cade's birthday!

After watching the nursery clean him we were able to meet him officially and hold him. As always, I sang to him, prayed over him and loved on him. His MiMi was so very proud of her new little grandson! What a joy and a blessing to be a grandmother. God knew at this age in life we would be perfectly content in the roll of grandparent. Loving them, speaking into their lives, encouraging them and believing in them were ways we can be what their parents can't. Creating a special bond and a special love, God designed a relationship between grandchildren and grandparents that only He could create. I am so grateful He did.

God has a way of knowing everything about us. Knowing we tire after our children are raised, He created grandchildren for us to enjoy, love, and spoil but then send home. The perfect arrangement I believe!

What about you? Has God given you grandchildren you can enjoy and call your own? Take time today to thank Him for this blessing. If you aren't there yet, thank Him anyway for the day they, too, will be yours!

*"May God Almighty bless you and make you fruitful and increase*
*your numbers until you become a community of peoples."*
*Genesis 28:3 (NIV)*

# PAIN RESTORED

Christmas time has always been my favorite time of the year. It was my late sister's too. When she died, it was extremely difficult, but the family made the best of the holiday season by bonding and supporting one another. For years I have dreaded, known, pushed aside and refused to accept that in days to come my 96-year-old grandmother, "*MaGump*" would have to leave us. Christmas was also her favorite time of year. Losing her would be devastating to me.

Two days before Thanksgiving 2008, "*MaGump*" went to be with the Lord. She finished her suffering, closed the last chapter and proudly stepped into the presence of her Savior. Selfishly, I mourn her passing. I mourn and grieve the idea that not only will I not see her again on this earth, but I will not be able to kiss her, hug her, talk to her, laugh with her or have her near me again.

I knew letting go would be hard. I had dreaded the pain and loneliness I would feel. I already knew the crippling effect from all the other loses in my lifetime. I also knew that God and His loving grace would see me through. One step at a time, one moment at a time and one breath at a time, my God would meet every need in the midst of my pain and suffering.

God, too, is fond of Christmas. His son was born to mankind. And like me, He later suffered and lost. Who better than the creator of life, the one who sent His only son to comfort me? Who better than the one who purposed His own son to die for you and me to minister to our painful needs? Personally, I can't think of anyone better!

Have you lost a loved one that has left you brokenhearted? Have you lived through a season that has caused you to dread, push aside, or refuse to accept the days to come when you loose someone very close to you? Take your pain or your anticipation of pain to the one who knows your hurt. Allow God to minister to your broken places. Let Him take your grief today. Let Him be your comforter like no other can possibly be!

*"For the Lamb at the center of the throne will be their Shepherd;*
*He will lead them to springs of living water.*
*And God will wipe every tear from their eyes."*
*Revelation 7:17 (NIV)*

# THE BATTLES AND THEIR SCARS

*I* have never really thought of it as such but it's true. I am a fighter. I am a warrior. I am called to the battlefield as a believer in the Gospel of Christ. I do battle daily and I will continue to do so until Christ calls me home.

My individual battle scars speak truth. Whether external or internal I have scars that reveal the individual encounters this journey of life has taken me on. Whether scars from surgery, a fall, or another mishap of some kind, each circumstance leaves behind it's own unique and lasting mark. Our battles in life aren't easy. They are meant to challenge the simplicity of our time here. Webster's dictionary defines the word battle as, "combat between opposing forces." Some of my personal battles have involved illness verses health, open spaces verses the confines of four walls and standing tall verses hitting the ground. No matter which one I face though, there is the battle of challenge. My senses, my emotions, my feelings, and my knowledge are all stirred up. Perhaps the most I find challenging however, is my faith. The faith that grows from every fight I come up against.

There are numerous, uncountable times God has been my Great Physician. Although wounds do consequently occur, the healing is ultimately what matters the most. The wisdom, the character building, and the firsthand moments I share totally with my creator, are worth every single one. His healing hand holds mine. His tender heart feels like mine. His incredible presence captivates me. Every battle I fight, here on earth, has already been won. It was in the battle of sin verses sacrifice that God gave His only Son to take on our every experience. Who better fit to escort us through than the Almighty God, our Father? For He has seen, experienced, and overcome every battle known to man.

What about you? Do you have scars that have never healed? Are you perhaps facing a battle in your present days? Are you weary from your fight? Rest assured there is one who has felt your pain firsthand. Our Heavenly Father wants to see you through. He wants to be your weapon so to finish the war His way. The question is, will you let Him? The truth is, you'll never win without Him.

*"I have told you these things, so that in me you may have peace.*
*In this world you will have trouble. But take heart!*
*I have overcome the world."*
*John 16:33 (NIV)*

# ANOTHER STEP FORWARD

*T*he ministry road for me has continually been a rewarding and unbelievable adventure. It has been my heartbeat since 1996. Over the years many opportunities have crossed my path but some required a minister's license I did not possess. Praying, I asked the Lord to help me acquire a license to enable me to minister in other areas. One day, not even focusing on my plea, I received an e-mail from a local Pastor friend who taught with me at school. Not knowing my prayer or my desires, He was inquiring about those interested in being ordained as ministers. I was completely awestruck! God had indeed heard my prayer and answered unlike I would have never imagined.

After twelve weeks of study, I traveled to Baltimore Washington with our class for the official ordination ceremony. The service included other ministerial, elder and pastoral candidates from across the country. Dressed in our black attire, we entered the sanctuary. During the processional, all I could feel was complete humility that the Lord had chosen me for this position. I knew I had been obedient regardless of my failures in life!

Once seated, candidates were escorted to the front of the church to stand before our Pastor and Bishop. Immediately, in their presence, the Spirit of the Lord filled me! My pastor laid hands on me and prayed a prayer of dedication for the ministry in which God had called me. In that very moment, I knew, without a shadow of a doubt, this was what God had created me for. It was truly an honorable and breathtaking moment.

Since my ordination, I have indeed been able to go places I never dreamed I would go. Visiting prisons, ICU units and performing marriage ceremonies, God has used me in many mighty ways. I am proof that if He purposes a plan in your life, He will do what it takes to realize that plan. Even if you don't understand how, He will do it!

What about you? Have you been obedient to the calling God has on your life or have you chosen to ignore His leading? Take time today to listen to where God wants to take you. Take time today to commit to the plan He has specifically written for your life.

*"'You are my witnesses,' declares the Lord, 'and my servant whom I have chosen,*
*so that you may know and believe me and understand that I am He. Before*
*Me no god was formed, nor will there be one after me.'"*
*Isaiah 43:10 (NIV)*

# THE LAST LAUGH

On Tuesday, November 22, 2009, my grandmother went to be with the Lord. She lived an extremely eventful, wonderful ninety-six years. With a very exhausted body, she was unable to hold on to life any longer.

My grandmother, MaGump, was a "hoot." She was a witty woman who spoke words of wisdom through encouragement, humor and down right honesty. Sometimes you could definitely say she was a sassy woman and a little on the bossy side! Most all the time though, she enjoyed just having fun and laughing!

MaGump was a resident in a local nursing home the day she passed away. By this time she was nearly completely bedridden just like many others on her hall. My mother and father were there with her when she took her last breaths. Sad to see her go, we were all grateful that she did not have to suffer any longer. Her last year of her life had been very challenging.

Shortly after she died, my parents sat with her awaiting the funeral home to arrive and take her body. My dad sat in a chair with his head propped against the wall and like millions of times before he dosed off to sleep. Suddenly, without warning the fire alarm went off. Jumping higher than he'd probably jumped in a decade, my daddy rose to his feet to see what the commotion was all about. This was the day. This was the moment. This was the hour. Following the guidelines for the mandatory monthly fire drill, every patient had to be escorted outside. Everyone except MaGump! She had to stay put. My poor parents had to stay put with her as the staff secured the building. To say the least, this just was not the greatest time to practice fire drill safety. Especially for my mom and dad! If I know my grandmother though, she would have laughed hysterically! In fact, I know she did have the last laugh!

Life has a way of sneaking up on us sometimes. Sometimes it sneaks up in the oddest ways. Indeed it did for my father and mother! The unpredictable, unexpected things we endure however never surprise God! He is ready and willing to see us through. In fact, I can assure you many times He laughs with us too. I do know He does with me!

What about your life? Do you expect Him in your daily adventures? Do you know He's with you every minute of every day? Take time today to step back and see where He needs to be involved in your life. Who knows, the laughter just might take the stress and unneeded pressure right off of you!

*"And I heard a voice from Heaven say 'Write this: Blessed are the dead who die in the Lord from now on. Yes, says the Spirit, they will rest from their labor, for their deeds will follow them!"*
*Revelation 14:13 (NIV)*

# THIRTY-FIVE YEARS LATER

*R*oswell Elementary School in Roswell Georgia was where I spent many years as a student from kindergarten to seventh grade. In my seventh grade year, I was chosen to be a school patrol. Grades, leadership skills and my overall personality qualified me for the position. Each morning and afternoon, our job was to patrol the halls and stairways in the school. We were to make sure students didn't run or act inappropriately while getting to their classes. I remember feeling so important in that roll of being a patrol!

Because of our outstanding service to the school and good grade averages, we were rewarded with a trip to Washington, D.C. It was the first time for me to actually go on a trip without my parents. I was so excited!

We rode a bus from the school to the train station in Atlanta, GA. After boarding, we traveled for a day and a half. We slept in our reclining seats and ate our meals in a small dining hall area on the train. Traveling to our destination was a thrilling experience within itself! After arriving in D.C., we toured the city in its entirety and to this day, I can still remember every historical place we visited. It was the most fantastic week! I will never forget it!

Thirty-five years later, I traveled back to the Nation's Capital. Standing in the very spots that I stood when I was a seventh grader was just so incredible for me. Even more so was sharing my earlier experiences with my own eighteen-year-old daughter. Together, my daughter and I stood on the very sites I stood alone so many years earlier. As I reminisced about that trip so many years ago, I told my daughter of all the many things I experienced all those years before and how so much had changed. It truly was a great moment in time for both of us!

Our lives are filled with rich history as well. Sharing stories with our children and grandchildren will ensure that they will be passed on to their children as well. Preserving and sharing the evidence of who we are and where we've been will inspire our generations to come. Our lives may not be as well known as the Father's of our country, but I want to ensure a Godly heritage is left by me for my family. I want more than anything for our future family to believe in the God that we believe in and trust today.

Our loving God prepared His people for the coming Messiah and because of that, I believe today. Now, the very seeds I plant in my own children will result in a fruitful harvest in years to come! Future Christian family members are what I pray to have.

What about you? Do you have a Godly heritage you will leave to your children? Will you be able to share your life story and how God was woven into it? Take time today to know that your belief in God will be apparent in your future family. Take time to prepare the way for those family members you will never even know.

*"You shall not bow down to them or worship them; for I, the Lord your God,*
*am a jealous God, punishing the children for the sin of the parents to the third*
*and fourth generation of those who hate me, but showing love to a thousand*
*generations of those who love me and keep my commandments."*
*Deuteronomy 5:9-10 (NIV)*

# SHE SHALL BE CALLED BLESSED

From the minute I found out I was to be a grandmother, I already knew what I wanted to be called. "MiMi" was my chosen identity. I had selected it for all of my grandchildren to call me. Why you ask? When I was growing up, my cousin's grandmother was also "MiMi." She was a remarkable and classy woman. I remember going to MiMi and Poppie's house with my cousin. It had an upstairs that had an incredible balcony. When looking over that balcony into the den, you could see that amazingly beautiful pool through the glass windows. I was sure I was one of the luckiest girls to ever have been invited to such an extravagant home.

Throughout the years, I saw MiMi age as we all do. She never looked a day older though. What I mean is, she was always beautiful and as classy as ever. Although, as an adult, I wish I could have had the opportunity to get to know her better. Moving around the country kept me from remaining close to anyone in my hometown. Her love for all kinds of people, places and things was something that set her apart. Not because it made her who she was, but because it allowed her to live life with total satisfaction. When I think about it now, she was always an inspiration to me. The interesting thing, however, is I'm not really so sure she even ever knew it. From a distance I could always see she was an extraordinary woman.

Being a grandmother, like that of my own grandmother, is a very special position. I don't take the role lightly. In fact, I believe, the family's legacy comes from a grandmother. The stories told, the traditions enforced, the passion for a Godly life and the first lady herself seemingly embeds the importance of one's heritage. I want to be that woman. Just as my grandmother and my children's grandmother have done for me and my children, and "MiMi for my cousin, I also want to be that influence for my own grandchildren. I want to be a legacy especially with my name. A one-of-a-kind Godly woman is who I want to be. "MiMi" is my name. . .

Have you given thought to what you will be called by your grandchildren and beyond? What is it that sets you apart? What is it about your walk with the Lord that you want your legacy to portrait? Ponder the future today. Think carefully what you want to leave behind in the story of your name. . . .

*"A good name is more desirable than great riches;*
*to be esteemed is better than silver or gold."*
*Proverbs 22:1 (NIV)*

# HIS OWN SPECIAL TALENT

*M*y oldest son was just not much of a football player. However in his younger years, his dad was. Sometimes as parents, we are guilty of seeing our children the way we see ourselves. We were guilty when it came to our child.

My son played on his first football team when he was seven. Several of his friends played so he was willing to try it. Each week he had to weigh in at 70 pounds. Being a healthy young man, towards the end of the season it became much more difficult. Having to eat healthier foods, drink more water and increase his work out, caused a good weigh in so he could play. Most of the time, however, he was just as happy on the sidelines. His dad and I loved to watch him play. Faithfully at every game we cheered him and his teammates on. His dad practiced with him at home and taught him what he could about his love for the game. Although my son enjoyed football and rooted for his fellow peers, he just wasn't as enthusiastic about being on the field himself. The bench was much less painful!

Even in the eighth grade, he tried again by joining the football team. Enduring grueling summer practices, he confessed the game was simply not his strength. In fact, he was not a sportsman at all!

What he soon did discover was his love for music. I, being a vocal major, had never forced my love for music on my children. It was simply a gift God had instilled inside of him. Messing around on the drums, he realized his skill for this instrument. Buying him his own set, he became increasingly rehearsed. Music was his true passion.

When my son became a father, he also had a son. Not only did he sing to him in the womb but when he was born. Fortunately, his little boy also loves the drums. He even had a child-sized set. Gifted like his dad, my grandson loves being a drummer!

God is faithful to instill gifts and talents in all of us. He is faithful to encourage, enhance, grow, and expand our gifts. It's up to us to ask Him. It's our responsibility to perfect what He's given us and use them for His kingdom.

What talent has God gifted to you? Has He been faithful to grow you or have you perhaps never invested in your gifts? Take time today to thank Him for what He's placed in you. Thank Him today for entrusting you with the talents He's so graciously given you.

*"We have different gifts, according to the grace given to each of us.*
*If your gift is prophesying, then prophesy in accordance with your faith."*
*Romans 12:6 (NIV)*

# A BITTERSWEET DAY

*I* talked myself into making this a wonderful day instead of one of sadness. It could have very easily been sad if we'd let it be; we just chose differently. My baby girl was leaving the nest to go away to college.

When we arrived, the campus personnel were swarming like flies. Former students were everywhere directing, helping and guiding people to their destinations. We unloaded my daughter's belongings, placed them on the sidewalk and waited to check-in. Once check-in was complete we loaded the elevators with tons of her stuff and headed to her new dorm room. Seventh floor, room 1717, was her new home away from home. She was so excited. Actually, we all were for her!

Just because we weren't going to allow it to be a sad day didn't mean our emotions weren't stirred up. The room became very claustrophobic when you crammed furniture and family members into these small quarters. Doing our best to cope, we successfully helped her unpack and settle in to her new temporary place.

Leaving wasn't so easy, but it was a must. Closing the door on the past and opening a new door to the future allows for such a needed change. As our days move onward, our steps must move that direction as well. It won't be easy, but it is necessary. The circle of life allows for new beginnings, new hopes and new dreams. The past is a great reminder of the lessons learned and it can remain in our hearts forever. Today we say good-bye to what's behind and look forward to the days ahead. In time, this too shall pass. Up ahead, there will again be new doors, new chapters and new beginnings all awaiting our arrival. Moving forward, however, I am just grateful I have a God who walks with me all the way.

Where are you in your season of life? Are you living in the present with change on the horizon or have you just stepped into your tomorrow? Take time today to stop for a moment and evaluate your steps. Making sure you are headed in the right direction, thank God for His presence to guide you. Thank Him today for allowing the newness in your future. Tomorrow is just around the bend. . . .

*"But when He, the Spirit of truth, comes, He will guide you into all truth. He will not speak on*
*His own; He will speak on what He hears and He will tell you what is yet to come."*
*John 16:13 (NIV)*

# THE WHISTLE

From the beginning of my childhood, I can remember my daddy and his whistle. No matter where my sister and I were we knew that sound! His whistle was unique. It was also very loud. Anyone who heard him sound off never forgot his call.

Back in the days when I grew up, we did ramble around but our parents trusted we would be safe. We could have ventured to the woods behind the house, the neighbors home or just in the yard playing but we knew when we were called that we had to come running! Unlike today, my parents didn't worry about my sister and I getting lost. Whenever we did venture off we were always immediately reunited when we heard my daddy call. With volume, force and a piercing sound, his whistle was the one thing we knew we had to obey. If not, a belt, a switch or possibly a backhand would greet us when we finally decided to show up!

As a teenager, I was so embarrassed by that whistle. It wasn't like the sound of it could blend in with all the other parents that summoned their children. Oh no, my daddy's call was clearly amplified to the max. I was mortified when I heard him call. Surely he realized the dread from his teenage daughters! In fact, my sister and I pleaded with him to devise another way of getting our attention. Our efforts were vetoed. The whistle stayed and we came running as usual!

Just after moving out of my parent's house to be married, dad could no longer whistle. Due to some unforeseen dental issues it made it impossible for him to sound off with his signature call. Strangely enough, I missed it! When grandchildren and great grandchildren were coming around a few years later, my dad began to holler like he once whistled. Now, the children holler like he does. Although his whistle may be history, his unique holler isn't!

God has a way of calling His children too. Once a child of God, you recognize His call. No matter the distance you are from Him, you know what it sounds like to hear His voice. No matter how long it's been since you've been near enough to hear His whisper, you seem to always recognize the sound of His call. No matter how far, we can always come running back to our Father!

How long has it been since you've heard the Father calling for you? Have you gone the other direction or have you immediately run into His arms? Take time today to thank Him for the loving, forgiving, nurturing daddy He is. Take time today to recognize the sound of His voice.

*"The gatekeeper opens the gate for him, and the sheep listen to his voice.*
*He calls his own sheep by name and leads them out."*
*John 10:3 (NIV)*

# IN A MATTER OF MINUTES!

On Sunday morning, May 1, 2010, my husband and I prepared to go to church like any other Sunday morning. It was raining as predicted in the local forecast and flood warnings were issued. Like most, though, we didn't pay too much attention to the warnings. As the intensity of the rain increased, my husband decided to walk to the basement just to make sure there were no leaks. Fortunately he did because when he reached the bottom of the steps, there was water flowing in from everywhere! The 3,000 square foot area was under four inches of water! He yelled for me and we began opening the doors and sweeping out the rain as hard as we could. The more we swept, the more the water came in it seemed. Calling a friend, we retrieved a water pump that helped get most of the water out into the yard instead of in our home.

Fortunately, there was no damage to our house. A few cardboard boxes and papers were submersed in water but nothing a little air wouldn't dry. Unfortunately for many others downtown, the story was much worse. That same morning, the single largest disaster to hit Middle Tennessee since the Civil War destroyed downtown Nashville; twenty-five minutes from our home. Torrential downpours caused the Cumberland River to rise 13 feet above flood stage. More than 30 people were killed and it turned out to be one of the most expensive natural disasters in U.S. history to date! There was an estimated $1 billion in damage.

Although our situation was not nearly the magnitude of the downtown flood area, it was still unbelievable to witness the forceful water in complete control. Within seconds, the waters rose to an unbelievable level with no regard of who or what was in its path! That day was one our family will always remember. It will go down in history!

There is another day that will, too, go down in history. Judgment Day. In this time God's oath will be proclaimed. His hand of judgment will be like that of the mighty waters and destruction will be prominent. Those that have chosen to deny His Holy name and proclaim evil will surely be dealt with. It will be a horrifying day!

Fortunately, it's not too late. God is still willing to take you in, clean you up, and make you an heir of His kingdom. The choice is yours. Take time today to examine your life. Are you willing to sacrifice it all to live in ways of the wicked or will you allow God to change you to be white as snow? God will never force your decision. You can guarantee, He will let you decide!

*"God swears against the arrogance of Jacob: 'I'm keeping track of their every last sin.' God's oath will shake earth's foundation, dissolve the whole world into tears. God's oath will sweep in like a river that rises, flooding houses and lands, And then recedes, leaving behind a sea of mud."*
*Amos 8:7 & 8 (The Message)*

# THE LIVING WALKING AWAY

Over the course of my lifetime, I've been forced to say good-bye to many loved ones. Literally, I've buried more than I care to count. Even at the half waypoint of my life, the age of 50, I had lost at least half of my family. From grandparents, parents-in-law, brother-in-laws, a sister, miscarriages, best friends, aunts, uncles and cousins. I always accepted that death is a natural part of life. Yes, you do have to walk out the grieving process. Eventually, though, your heart is temporarily healed. Knowing I will see them again certainly helps pad the pain!

Now for the first time, experiencing the loss of someone that has turned away from you is a whole "different bird." It's like knowing you are about to drown but you still have some life left in you. Enough life to reach up, take a breath, and sink back under. You actually do finally realize though, you will never totally drown. You'll only loose your way for a little while. Underneath the mucky water, your sight is blurred, your way is dark and your breath is temporarily sucked out of you. The journey seems too hard to handle. The weight on your shoulders is way overbearing. And the roller coaster of emotion is intense and takes many turns and dips.

Jesus, too, knew the pain of loss. He even wept when Lazarus died. With His family, He felt the tremendous agony they each were experiencing. And people walking away from you? He's also a master at that one! Throughout history, people turned on Him. They followed Him while He ministered. They saw firsthand the miracles He performed. They worshiped in the temple with Him. Suddenly, like they'd never even known Him, they betrayed Him. They rejected Him. They finally crucified Him.

As I walk this lonely road of rejection and pain, I have to continually remember there is one who knows my trial. In fact, unlike me, He died from His rejection. I won't!

What about you? Do you have a burden you need someone to hear today? Know that the Lord of Lord's and the King of King's knows your pain. And never forget. . . . He died because of it!

*"He was despised and rejected by mankind, a man of suffering, and familiar with pain. Like one from whom people hide their faces He was despised, and we held Him in low esteem."*
*Isaiah 53:3 (NIV)*

# THE HANGING

For many, decorating the Christmas tree is an event that is quick and easy, but for me it's not exactly how my vision perceives it. I love Christmas. I also love decorating! In preparing for this timely event, I have spent countless Christmas's purchasing just that perfect ornament or saving one attached to a Christmas package. Over the course of time many new decorations have adorned our tree. Several have been gifts from special friends who knew how important ornaments were to me. Some were ones that caught my attention and reminded me of a place, person or time in my past. Most of them, however, were usually donated to the cause by one of our children who had so creatively made them at school during their holiday preparations. Because of the boxes of ornaments I now possess, I have had to divide them into three separate trees! Each room that holds a tree casts it's own special story from every limb!

Not just anything can hang from my tree though. I want each ornament to have its own special beauty, its own special story, and its own special place. As I unpack each box to begin the hanging, my mind still races back to that event, year, or occasion that particular decoration represents. Hours will pass as I reminisce the moments of Christmas's past. By the time my decorating is complete I have relived my years from childhood until present!

I am so grateful for my Christmas trees. Nearly every year of my life is represented on a branch. From childhood to teenage years, from marriage to motherhood, from children growing up, to those loved ones that have passed on, I love to remember the days of old. More than anything, I am grateful for the opportunity once a year to relive my life's events in each decoration. Some memories good, while others very painful, I still cherish them all. As each year passes, I await in anticipation for that special hour when I can again, decorate my tree.

What about you? Have you special memories you hang in your tree each year? Have you by chance forgotten to take the time to recall the moments from your past as you hang each ornament? Take time today, to thank God for the memories you hold so dear, or begin today building memory reminders through your tree ornaments this very Christmas!

*"Your statutes are my heritage forever; they are the joy of my heart."*
*Psalm 119:111 (NIV)*

# THE NAIL SALON

*J*ust after my best friend moved from Nashville, Tennessee to Stillwater, Oklahoma, I flew out for a girl's weekend visit. It was going to be hard to live without her. Life brings about change at times and I would have to learn to live with this change!

After flying most of the day, my friend picked me up from the airport and took us for an evening of pampering. Her soon to be daughter-in-law joined us as my friend and I decided to finish our long day with a pedicure! Best friends and pedicures are a match in Heaven!!!

Relaxing in the pedicure chairs was simply divine but when an added remote control chair with a back massage comes along with it, there just are no words! Trying to keep our composure in those chairs without falling asleep, we talked, shared and caught up on our lives after our un-welcomed separation.

Before we knew it, our pedicures were done. Still waiting on my friends' daughter-in-law to have a manicure, the owner of the establishment encouraged us to stay in our chairs, repeat the glorious back massage and wait until the manicure was complete. As we sat and waited, my friend and I were immediately sucked into a state of sleepiness. With eyelids heavy along with the repetitive massaging motions addressing our backsides, it was "all she wrote". We were done for and we didn't even realize it! We had been seduced to a slumber in a public establishment as grown adults! Not just a short nap but a disgustingly obvious one that certainly should not have been permitted in a public place! When I finally came to from my semi-comatose state, I quickly regained my composure and shook my friend awake. We were both mortified! Briskly we wiped the saliva from our face and chin, poofed our bed-head hair and gathered our belongings. Fortunately, there were no new customers in the shop to admire our uncouth disposition! Without question, we were both totally humiliated at the likes of our uncontrolled, unladylike, mannerless configuration.

How many times have you begun with one intention and ended up completely sidetracked or seduced. Not enough rest or perhaps caught off guard; the enemy can quickly derail our intended motive. He can lead us down the wrong track even in the most pertinent place. Luring us with his enticing ways, we can be sucked into his trap unless we are rested, alert and prepared to battle against his seductive schemes. Full of ulterior motives we must be prepared to rise above the temptation the enemy throws our way. We have to always be on guard with readiness to do battle with the power we possess from the indwelling Holy Spirit!

What is it today you battle with? Are there areas in your life you need to address so you may better prepare to battle? Take time today and ask God to reveal those areas. Ask Him to give you wisdom on how to be a better soldier so you may fight in this earthly battle called "life".

*"Be alert and of sober mind. Your enemy the devil prowls around like*
*a roaring lion looking for someone to devour."*
*1 Peter 5:8 (NIV)*

# TRADITION CARRIED ON

*I*n our family, tradition is important. Not only to my husband and our children, but me. You might say we have spoiled them more than we realize!

In our household, Christmas morning is a wonderful time. Santa visits all the children that still live at home. No matter if they are newborn or in college, the same rule applies. Easter is the same way. Baskets filled with goodies and spring attire awaits the receiver on Easter morn.

My son left home first and then married. When he did, as the rules state, he forfeited his rights as a receiver of Santa on Christmas or a basket filled with goodies on Easter. My middle daughter also sacrificed these amenities when she moved out into a house of her own.

When my baby girl left for college the first year, she began thinking about the excitement of growing up, leaving the nest and getting an apartment. Although she loved living at home and loves us, she always dreamed of the benefits of adulthood. I suppose as the day approached for her departure to college she pondered the upcoming changes in her life. She remembers the rules. Calling one afternoon, she said, "*Mom, I was just wondering if you could tell me again the rules about Christmas and Santa?*" "*Sure,*" I said. "*If you leave home to live on your own or get married, you no longer are entitled to Santa. Your gifts will be wrapped and placed under the tree for family opening time only.*" "*OK,*" she said. "*I just wanted to make sure I understood.*" "*OK,*" I said chuckling at her childlike enquiry.

A few days later, I received another call. "*Mom?*" she said. "*Can you please explain to me the rules about the Easter Bunny. I was just thinking about spring and I thought about my Easter basket.*" A little startled, I said, "*Sure. The deal is the same. If you move into your own place or you get married and move, you forfeit the Easter Bunny's gifts.*" Somewhat relieved, my daughter said, "*OK good. Just so you know, I am not moving until I graduate from college. I don't want to loose one year of getting my gifts from Santa or the Easter bunny!*"

Completely surprised by her call, I couldn't help but laugh! Even though she was 19, I was so humored by her childlike thoughts. I realized that even though my daughter lived in her college dorm, there was still a part of her that remains with us. Knowing she still wants to be our little girl until she absolutely has to give up all of her childlike ways is such a relief for me as a mother. It probably always will be!

God has a way of allowing us time to adjust to things. He's there to hold our hand, reassure us and walk with us through the changes in our lives. Good or bad, He never fails. No matter the season, the celebration, the holiday or the event, God celebrates with us. He is our Father and knows just how much we need Him. No matter, life isn't the same without Him! Take time today to thank God for always walking beside you. Thank Him for being your constant abiding friend!

*"Praise the Lord. Praise God in His sanctuary; praise Him in His mighty heavens.*
*Praise Him for His acts of power; praise Him for His surpassing greatness.*
*Let everything that has breath praise the Lord"*
*Psalm 150:1, 2 & 6 (NIV)*

# PEE YEW

*B*eing a native Georgia girl, I soon discovered that wildlife in Tennessee was somewhat different from the neck of woods I was raised in. Back home, you could always find a dead possum in the middle of the road. It was ridiculous. There were songs sung about them, jokes cracked because of them, and even a southern recipe made up for them. They called it "Possum Stew." (original, huh?) Those stinking varmints were everywhere!

In Tennessee however, I quickly learned the number one road kill is the skunk. Yes, and you never even need to see one. There is no mistake! You know from miles away one has just expired! When one of those varmints lives have been taken, they come back to haunt you. . .literally! There scent is atrocious!

One February evening, a couple of friends and I were returning home from an evening dinner in town. Almost to my subdivision, we saw a skunk about to cross the road just in the distance. Knowing the precautionary measures to avoid an encounter, my friend slowed down giving the rodent ample time to acquire it's own lane instead of sharing ours. Feeling pretty confident the coast was clear, we sped up and continued on our way. For some strange reason, all of a sudden that skunk did a one eighty, came barreling back across the road and headed straight towards our car. Swerving and nearly killing us to try and miss the darn thing, unfortunately, that did not happen. Like a huge sewer explosion, the skunk was split wide open by the force of her wheels and muffler. Instantly, we knew that skunk had left its mark. It's one thing to smell one from a far off but it's another to smell one on top of you! Nearly choking to death, we finally pulled in my driveway and ran for the house. Even the air in my home soon reeked of our disastrous encounter. Needless to say, a professional car cleaning and deodorizer was required to restore the natural smell of her vehicle!

Fortunately, God is in the refreshing business. Taking our unpleasant circumstances in His hand, He can restore them into an even better scent. It's in our obedience to finally give Him reign that He can freshen the air and rebuild our ruins into greater and more effective learning experiences. Eventually, He gives us an opportunity to share with another and perhaps spare them the same odor we endured.

What is it today that needs to be sniffed out in your life? Are their circumstances, behaviors or attitudes you need to hand over to God? Take time today to smell the odor of the problem areas in your life. Hand them over to the only one who can eliminate the stench and sweeten your life!

*"But seek first His Kingdom and His righteousness, and all these things will be given*
*to you as well. Therefore do not worry about tomorrow, for tomorrow will*
*worry about itself. Each day has enough trouble of its own."*
*Matthew 6:33 & 34 (NIV)*

# CLIMBING THAT LADDER

From the time my husband and I married, his goal was to climb the ladder of success. Not only for our future but also for our family. As our babies were born, company transfers gave continuous opportunities to move about every two years. I have to admit it was exciting having new houses that never got old. It was also quite refreshing continually meeting and making new friends. Friends that will last a lifetime!

Finally after the tenth move, we settled in one of my favorite homes. The city reminded me so much of my hometown in Georgia. White House, Tennessee was a quant little town with extremely friendly people! For the first time in our 15 years of marriage, we were determined to settle down for at least five years. That five, however, has turned into thirteen. Memories good and some bad adorned our established home. In fact, for our baby, it was the only home she ever knew. We experienced life and death there. We entertained joy as well as sorrow there. It's amazing the things that can happen in thirteen years. From building up to tearing down; from loving intensely to loving no more; from hanging on to letting go; from starting over to ending completely. Life was indeed lived in that house. It was lived to the fullest. And just like life, things change. Time changes things and us as well.

I thank God for the memories in that old house. I still think about what's there even though we've sold and moved again. I do love my new home, mind you, but I will treasure what has been left behind. A new day; a fresh start; the story of our life has been saturated with the presence of love. Oh the sweet fragrance of the life we've lived. That sweet smell takes us back in time to seasons of old. Moments and memories that will remain forever no matter where we lay our heads. And our new house, will continue to collect new memories, new traditions, new friends, and new seasons all its own.

What about you? Have you a place called home? Whether one of your own or one from your childhood, are there places with memories you will treasure forever? Thank God today that He allows us to remember. Thank Him, too, that we can carry a piece of our history around in the "Hall of Fame" we call our mind.

*"The Lord will command the blessing upon you in your storehouse and in*
*all that you undertake, and He will bless you in the*
*land which the Lord your God gives you."*
*Deuteronomy 28:8 (AMP)*

# COMPARING ROLES

My husband has basically been in the same profession since our marriage in 1979. I, on the other hand, have made many job changes throughout our lives. With his job transfers to other cities and me having babies, it was impossible for me to stay with a job continuously. In comparing his picture perfect record to mine, I had somehow lost sight of just where I was trying to even go. Had I gotten lost in the transition of the many positions I had mastered or did I require every single bit of experience I had acquired to date?

Finally, the Lord showed me a recap of the womanly role that He carved out for me. Caught up in the disappointment of an unhealthy comparison to that of my husband, God quickly reeled me in. His purpose, His intention, and His direction was never meant to be compared to the role He appointed to my spouse. In fact, He clearly had a completely different plan for me than the one He had laid out for my husband!

While God and I talked, He kindly reminded me of the interesting areas of life He allowed me to live. From housewife to mother, from teacher to employee, from leader to witness, God had continuously given me opportunity after opportunity. Each season of my life has been preciously spent chipping away just the part of me God wanted for His very own. Each day was numbered, every moment predestined, and every hair on my head was counted. Without the challenges, disappointments, accomplishments, failures and successes I would have missed all where God wanted me to walk! Without all of my accomplishments, I could never have reached the place in life He now has taken me to. Looking at who I am today is dictated by every experience and job I worked on yesterday.

What about you? Have you ever felt the frustration of comparison? Have you ever compared yourself with that of your spouse or another? Ask God today to remind you where you have been. Ask Him today to give you a recap of the way He's guided you. Thank Him today for the opportunities He has given you.

*"It was He who gave some to be apostles, some to be prophets, some to be evangelists, and some to be pastors and teachers, to prepare God's people for works of service, so that the body of Christ may be built up until we all reach unity in the faith and in the knowledge of the Son of God and become mature, attaining to the whole measure of the fullness of Christ."*
*Ephesians 4:11&12 (ESV)*

# LIVING OUT YOUR LOSSES

*L*earning to live without is costly. A better definition is sacrifice! With sacrifice, there is pain involved in one aspect or another.

There have been numerous times in my life where losing has been my greatest sacrifice. Whether a sister, a best friend, a grandparent, a relative, or a treasured pet living without severely hurts! Many times I have cried myself to sleep. Many times I remembered until it hurt too much to remember anymore. Physically speaking, my heart literally shattered into pieces. Many days those very pieces cut like shattered glass deep within my being. I became so overwhelmed with the pain of loss that I didn't know what I was going to do with myself.

Over the years, I have learned that pain continues to come my way. There is no stopping it. There is no preparing for it. It happens and it will continue. I do believe that even though our circumstances, our trials and our sacrifices may be different, our past experiences shape our ability to endure the things ahead. Molded by our history of misfortunes, we are able to remind ourselves of what to do and what not to do to survive yet another circumstance.

Through it all though, I am certain. Through it all, I am assured. Through it all, I simply know that God is in the comfort business. Instead of giving up on the old, God gently restores me to new. He's there through every move, every phase and every single progressive step to wholeness. In fact, He fills the holes with Himself to make me truly whole again.

What is it in you that you need restored? Will you reveal your brokenness to God so that He can put the pieces back in their perfect places? Lay your pieces in His hands. In exchange for your shattered mess, He will provide a beautiful and complete return. Trust in His restoration process today.

*"The Lord is my shepherd; I have everything I need. He lets me rest in green pastures. He lets me rest in green pastures. He leads me to calm water. He gives me strength. He leads me on paths that are right for the good of His name. Even when I walk through a very dark valley, I will not be afraid, because you are with me. Your rod and your walking stick comfort me."*
*Psalm 23:1-4 (NCV)*

# MY PRINCE

*A*s a little girl, like most, I dreamed of finding my prince, getting married, and having the most beautiful children. All my dreams came true!

In the summer after my senior year, I met my husband. We were very much attracted to one another and spent hours upon hours getting to know everything about one another. He came from a family of Christian parents with a Preacher as a father. I attended church with my family from the time I exited the womb. With a very strong Godly upbringing, I knew our beliefs in God were the same. For me, that was the most important thing to have in a man!

One of the things I always dreamed of was meeting the one who would love me so very much. I desired someone who supported who I was as a person and believed in me as much as my parents had always done.

I will never forget when my husband and I started dating and I remember that many times we could just silently sit together. Strangely, we would just stare into each other's eyes. We never said a word. It was as if our hearts, spirits and beings were just connected. For hours we'd only look at one another and never even move. We fell in love knowing God had joined us together forever!

Throughout the years, we have equally supported one another. Knowing the person God created us to be, we believed in one another. Different talents, different skills, different passions and different callings, God has used us to lift up the other and enhance the gifts, goals, and talents our Heavenly Father has instilled within us. Our differences have completed the other. Our strengths have fulfilled the other's weaknesses. Together we make a team. Together we are one!

Today makes 39 years since we met and 37 since we married. Our history has included absolutely wonderful times as well as times we'd like to completely forget. We have had good seasons and bad seasons. We may understand one another and then at times not. We determined when we married we would move forward loving each other 'til *death do us part.*" Today, we are still moving forward. Bottom line, we promised never to give up. Three beautiful children, a son-in-law, a daughter-in-law to be and three grandchildren are proof of how God has richly blessed us. He has indeed fulfilled the dreams He placed within us. He has joined the two of us. Until He calls us home, we are determined to finish this walk together!

What has God purposed in your life? Take time today to evaluate the blessings He has provided in your life. Thank Him for those relationships that are joined by Him!

*"A wife must stay with her husband as long as he lives. If he dies, she is free to marry anyone she chooses. She will, of course, want to marry a believer and have the blessing of the Master."*
*1 Corinthians 7:39 (The Message)*

# FINAL MOMENTS

*B*ecoming older tends to escort in the reality of the loss of loved ones near to us. Wanting to un-invite myself to this stage of life, I am forced to reconcile my differences, see man's life through God's perspective, and say goodbye to some so dear.

As a younger woman, death was known of but tucked away on the shelves of my mind. Unfortunately, I have tiptoed upon it and have been forced to face death's unexpected call for many of my family members and very close friends. The loss of my sister nineteen years ago intensified the force of this cycle. It's a day-to-day thing now to hear of the enemy's force through cancer, illness, or an accident targeting the ones I've loved.

Only four short years ago, my adopted sister and best friend God sent me after loosing my blood sister also died suddenly. Assaulted with emotion, I was devastated again. Thinking I just might have had an upper hand on those that seemed likely to be called home was the farthest thing from the truth! Thinking I couldn't live without her has proven to be something I have had to do! I never in a million years dreamed I would have to say goodbye to her before she said goodbye to me. Because I was twenty years older, I was sure I would have been able to bypass that pain. I was dead wrong!

I know my Lord and Savior holds the key to death and life, but it is human to fear the unknown. I admit my struggle with this earthly departure. I fear not where I am going. I fear not my Savior taking hold of my hand. I fear not the arrival into that beautiful city. Hesitantly though, I fear the pain that cripples me whenever I think of loosing another loved one to sudden death.

Like many other fears we must face, I boldly hand it over to God. Eventually, the creator will stroke my heart, fill my veins with peace and send me back to the day I am in. Graciously, He will remind me to live life to the fullest and allow Him the details of my own individual exit plan.

Are their stages of life you, too, dare not face? Are their fears that control your emotions while you stroll on the sidewalk of life? Take time today to allow God to intravenously fill you up with peace. Let Him gently stroke your heart while calming that fear within.

*"Your eyes saw my unformed substance; in your book were written,*
*every one of them, the days that were formed for me,*
*when as yet there was none of them."*
*Psalm 139:16 (ESV)*

# My Own Fire

Trials, challenges and problems are not something most people stand in line to receive. In fact, they most often cause much stress, anxiety and pressure for the natural man. Honestly, although they challenge our character defects, they also challenge our state of being!

Being called to the ministry took a tremendous toll on me. Unquestionably, sure of my passion for people that calling dared me to look deeper into God's Word, my soul and my drive as a woman. Trials, challenges and problems came with a vengeance. Seeking God with fervor of sorts eventually resulted in a vision within my spirit God engraved. I will guarantee you though visions take time. They also take determination and perseverance. Most often, there is no guarantee what they will require you to experience.

There is no question God has called me to minister. He has given me a desire to help others emotionally as well as spiritually. I can tell you it wasn't always easy enduring the days prior to God using my past to minister to people in my present. From death of family members and friends, deep depression, family addiction and financial loss, time eventually allowed healing and lessons were learned. Subsequently, God continues to use my firsthand wisdom, success and brokenness to minister where He saw me in the beginning of this journey called life.

Today I still seek seeing my specific dream come to reality. Experiencing my own concoction of trials, tribulations and heartaches, I know He has placed me in the role of exhorter and encourager for now. He allows me to equip others and be used as an instrument of reconciliation and restoration for His flock that so desperately need hope. I can honestly say I greatly anticipate the day my dream unfolds. The past remains in the past but today I am certain it was an essential tool in my ministry for today.

What about you? Are you in the midst of heartache and trial? Are you concerned your past has past? Trust God today that every piece of your story has a place. Expect today that He will place every moment, every adversity and every adventure in its exact position in your tapestry story and create the artistry He intended for your future.

*"Remember the former things, those of long ago; I am God, and there is no other; I am God, and there is none like me. I make known the end from the beginning, from ancient times, what is still to come. I say, "My purpose will stand, and I will do all that I please.""*
*Isaiah 46:9 & 10 (NIV)*

# UNANSWERED QUESTIONS

One morning in March of 1996, I awoke with that alarming, but familiar feeling that I've previously felt only four times in my life. My husband was out of town on a business trip that day so I was forced to uncover the mystery of my illness alone. I was certain something was wrong! Pinning the issue was what scared me the most. I hesitantly purchased a pregnancy test and sat prayerfully awaiting the results. As a positive mark rapidly exposed the screen, my heart skipped a beat. In total disbelief, I cried out to God feeling sure in the fact that He would know what was happening. Having a baby was supposed to be impossible! My husband was the product of a vasectomy three years prior and up until then, the results had been foolproof. Somehow, someway, something had gone seriously wrong!

Determined to make sure the test was correct I immediately called a local walk-in clinic. Only a few short minutes after taking the test again the confirmation was correct. We were having another child. Reluctantly, I made a 911 call to my husband. Slipping out of his company meeting, I gently spilled the news. In shock as well, he assured me we would get through this unexpected turn of events as we had many others in the past!

Still in shock and totally surprised, a week later my first visit to the doctor was again one of non-preparation. My miracle baby's heartbeat had stopped. Again, the questions suddenly stacked up higher and higher. My parental emotions raged with grief. Excepting the unbelievable and then rejecting it's mark sent me into a mangled state of confusion.

Still today, I have no idea why God allowed me to conceive another child at my age. I still have no comprehension of how surgery after three years was suddenly undone. How was I to even remotely understand why that miracle baby would be given and just as quickly taken away? I am certain though that one day when I cross from this life to my eternal home I will have the joy of being greeted by two little children I have never known. Today I choose to wait in the hope that God does indeed have all of the answers. I wait in great anticipation when He tells me all I ever wanted to know.

What about you? Are there questions you need answers to? Ask Him today to prepare your heart. Know today that one day soon, the unknown will be revealed unveiling the answers to your life's puzzle.

*"Those who know your name will trust in you, for you,*
*Lord, have never forsaken those who seek you."*
*Psalm 9:10 (NIV)*

# THE LEAST I COULD DO FOR HIM

My upbringing moved me to become a member of the United Methodist Church at the age of thirteen. As denominational beliefs would have it, my parents christened me as a child. My decision to be born again, however, was something I had to do on my own in my heart.

When my husband and I had our second child we were drawn to join a local Baptist Church in our area. My husband was raised Baptist but becoming one was a huge change for me. One of the requirements to join the Baptist Church was not only to be a believer of Jesus Christ, (which we were) but to follow that decision in water baptism. Rebelliously, I fought that theory. I was not comfortable "*getting dunked*" at all! I was determined in my own beliefs that my parents had taken care of my baptism for me. If the truth be known, I was mad that they were telling me what I needed to believe and how I needed to believe it.

As the days went on, the more I struggled. I was honestly down right mad! I was so bothered that I couldn't even sleep! Finally, I called my former youth counselor and explained my dilemma. I knew she would understand. She did. In fact, she had also changed denominations. She not only joined the Baptist church but followed that decision in water baptism as well. I was shocked. I was now listening to her reasons why. That day, she asked me one of the most thought provoking questions I think I've ever been asked. She said, "The sacrifice that Christ made for you on the cross at Calvary was incredible. His sacrifice saved your life! The least you could do to show that you receive what He did for you is to be publically baptized." My heart stopped. My mind changed. I was so ashamed. I got it! I understood it! I wanted it! God had transformed my heart instantaneously in that moment. He changed the rhythm of my heartbeat that second to beat just like His.

The following Sunday, I was publically baptized. My husband was also. It was an amazing experience to fall back into that water dying to my old life and being raised back up again changed and made whole. Death. Burial. Resurrection.

What about you? Have you moments of rebellion where your head won't let your heart do what God may require of you? Have you listened to His promptings and your flesh act out the opposite? Ask Him today if there is something He requires of you to do in complete obedience to Him. Take time today to meet with your Father and know you are being all that you can be through Him.

*"As has just been said: "Today, if you hear His voice,*
*do not harden your hearts as you did in the rebellion."*
*Hebrews 3:15 (NIV)*

# THE EXCHANGE PARTY

2010 was a challenging year. Much opposition passed through the waters in my family's life and mine. Faithfully, however, God was with us. He never left our side! He placed so many special people in our lives that helped calm the storms. He used friends to intercede in prayer and be there when our family needed them the most. In thankfulness for the many He did use, I hosted a Christmas Dinner Party. It was a time to thank each one for the blessing they had been to my family and me.

The evening hosted 24 women from all different walks of life. From younger women to older, the guests arrived. With casseroles, desserts and vegetable dishes in hand, we gave thanks and enjoyed a lovely dinner together. Amazingly, many of the ladies had never met. Living in the same small town, it was hard to believe!

After dinner, we gathered in my living room and each woman introduced herself. After the introductions I read a devotional I had written sharing how important this time of year was to me. I shared how special each ornament was that hung on my Christmas tree. I told the women that every ornament had a story that related to my past through an event, person or place. It was special for me to share this tradition with my friends. My hope was that each year, as they decorated their tree, they would remember the many blessings they were afforded. Each friend brought an ornament to exchange and my hope was they would always remember the evening we shared together.

By night's end, every woman had a new memory in hand through the special ornament they received. New friends were made and for some, old friends were reunited. The past was remembered and a new future ready to begin. Laughter, hugs, tears but most of all love, was exchanged this night. The evening was exactly how I had pictured. It was a celebration of friends who had given a part of themselves to become just like family!

God's intensions are for us to lean on one another. He has created us for relationships. It is during the toughest times in life; He knows we will need a physical hug, word or deed to get us through. It's in our obedience to Him, that we are given the opportunity to be a blessing and in turn will be blessed by others.

What about you? Have you been obedient to be an extension of God's hands and feet this year? Has He used you to minister to a friend in need? Take time to thank Him for using you to bless another. Take time today to thank Him equally for allowing another to be a blessing to you!

*"How beautiful on the mountains are the feet of the messenger bringing*
*good news, telling Zion, "Your God reigns!"*
*Isaiah 52:7 (The Message)*

# WE REMEMBERED

The room was silent. The women were seated. The morning was our normal Friday-gathering day for Bible Study in my office. It had become a tradition of sorts that we gather to seek the face of God as a family. We were now a sisterhood. We were a spiritual unit joined by our hearts through God. We were Hope Center Ministries White House Women's Center.

Brokenness, failures, discontentment and disgusted wretchedness had brought every woman present to that room. Years of running, years of rebellion and years of disbelief had positioned them in a forcible place of surrender. Bound by the results of their past actions, these ladies were finally prepared to grasp hold of the one that could finally restore every ounce of their brokenness.

That day we didn't just read the Bible and recall the story, that day we were there with the disciples. As described in scripture, the women and I joined the twelve, with Jesus, in that Upper Room. We could hear the sweet voice of our Savior as He prepared His followers for His departure. We could see the faces of the men as they engaged their hearts. We could see their expressions as their eyes were captivated by every word that left the lips of their Savior.

Doing what Jesus asked that day of all believers, we remembered. In my ordinary little office that morning, the women and I broke bread. We remembered His body. We drank juice and remembered His shed blood. We were captivated and intoxicated by His presence.

Not only did we experience communion as a family, we experienced God. That day we purposefully sat and waited in great anticipation for Him to speak. We listened to His voice. We were changed in His presence.

How many times do we participate and yet the sacrament has become only a ritual? How often do we engage in the mystery of our religious beliefs for them to just become religion? How have we lost sight? How have we dared to forget the stillness of the hour Jesus spoke words that would pierce our hearts for generations and generations to come?

What about you? Have you waited lately? Have you sat in silence in the midst of God alone? In His very presence we are moved. We are changed. We are made whole. Take time today to be still so you may seek God and share in the remembrance of the price He paid for the forgiveness of your every sin!

*"In the same way, after supper He took the cup, saying,*
*"This cup is the new covenant in my blood; do this,*
*whenever you drink it, in remembrance of me."*
*1 Corinthians 11:25 (NIV)*

# MiMi and Pops

For those that do not have grandchildren, let me just tell you it's truly one of the most wonderful experiences in life! The feeling of being loved and being able to love in such a way as this is incredible. For those that haven't been blessed with any yet, just wait. It will change your life forever!

On June 27, 2007, our first grandson was born to our firstborn son. This precious baby boy was prayed for and was the start of a new chapter for us as grandparents.

In April of 2012, we became grandparents again. A precious baby girl was born to our middle daughter. Our new 'grandgirl' was as adored by us, just as was our grandson. She was going to be so spoiled and her momma made sure every outfit, every picture and every moment included a huge, oversized hair bow on her tiny head!

Then in June of 2014 we were again blessed with another precious grandbaby girl. She was born to my son. Our new grandbaby was adorable! She was assuredly another gift from God! My husband and I birthed one boy and two girls. That same pattern was being repeated in our grandchildren! That order originally began with my own set of siblings!

In my living room sits my grandmother's rocker. That rocker is precious to me. I honestly have no idea who all had been rocked in it before it came to be in my house. One of the things I love about it is it squeaks. It squeaks loud! It drives the rest of my family crazy, but interestingly enough it sooths all three of my grandbabies every time I rock them. It's our special time. It's our special bonding moment. That rocker rocks, and still does, each of my precious grandbabies!!

Our grandchildren mean the world to both my husband and me, as do their parents! I would have to say our grandchildren are pretty fond of us as well. Gathering, mingling and creating special memories are so important to our growing family. Every holiday, every birthday and whenever everyone is finally in town, we try and get the 'grands' together. Cousins making memories is so important! Reuniting indeed creates treasured moments in our family's history!

I believe God loves family time too. In fact, He loves spending time with His children. Creating us to multiply and be relational, family reunions are a must. Living our daily lives apart makes for great reunions and catch up gatherings!

What about you? Has your family tree grown branches? Have you stepped from parenthood to grandparenthood? Whether parents, grandparents or just siblings, take time to make time to come together. Take time to create new memories that you can treasure for the remainder of your days.

*"Children's children are a crown to the aged; and parents are the pride of their children."*
*Proverbs 17:6 (NIV)*

# MY SPIRITUAL DAUGHTER

*B*eing the director of a local women's center was one of the most rewarding yet gut-wrenching jobs I've ever had. Every woman admitted suffered from drug and/or alcohol addiction. Every hurt, habit or hang-up had certainly taken its toll on these ladies!

One February evening in 2013, a young woman transferred to our location from our other women's center. Suffering the consequences of some unwise choices her options were to return to jail or transfer locations. She chose to make the move but I can tell you it was under complete protest! She was not happy at all about her relocation!

Telling her family and friends good-bye, we left for White House with hopes of her beginning a deeper journey in her healing process. As we pulled onto the interstate, she quickly instructed me to take her directly to the Parthenon psychiatric hospital in Nashville. She was certain the grief and pain from her past and the recent, tragic death of her mom had driven her literally crazy! She begged me. She pleaded with me. She wanted someone, anyone, to make her pain just STOP! She was honestly in a desperate state!

That night was indeed the beginning of her recovery road. Over the next few months, we talked, we counseled, we cried, we laughed, we fought, we discussed, we planned, we dug up, we dove in and we did everything possible to revive the deadness from the aches and pains that haunted her. It was hard. It was excruciating at times! It was necessary in order to heal! Every day we worked on the issues at hand. We dealt with every situation that occurred, every emotion that welled up and every secret that she had buried.

Through God's healing power, we watched restoration take place. This woman was becoming a new creation. God was restoring her from the inside out and everything the enemy had stolen from her was being returned. Her choices had ultimately landed her at rock bottom but that bottom was quickly becoming her podium in which to testify.

Our journey together for those months created a bond that will forever be. Our time together will never be forgotten. Although she lost her natural mother, I have become her spiritual one. I am honored and I am so blessed by her! Having a front row seat to see God perform miracles before my very eyes is indescribable! God does have a way of meeting our every need!

Today, this young woman is still a huge part of the ministry. After graduation she served as the day and night manager and now counsels and leads the women in the daily operations. Her story of restoration offers HOPE for other ladies that so desperately need to be revived through Christ!

There is not a moment that goes by that we don't need God. Every tear, every hurt, every pain, every situation is important to Him. Often we will decide to rely on our own remedies and judgment when in fact, we have no earthly idea what we need to do. Our only saving grace comes from God alone!

What about you? Have you been in a place of desperation? Have you hit rock bottom of sorts? Allow God to come to your aide. Let Him administer comfort, healing and true restoration in your mangled mess. Allow Him to breathe new breath into your dead, lifeless condition.

> *Then He said to me, "Prophesy to these bones and say to them, 'Dry bones, hear the word of the Lord! This is what the Sovereign Lord says to these bones: I will make breath enter you, and you will come to life. I will attach tendons to you and make flesh come upon you and cover you with skin; I will put breath in you, and you will come to life. Then you will know that I am the Lord.'"*
> *Ezekiel 37:4-6 (NIV)*

# OUR TUESDAY NIGHTS

*E*very Tuesday morning, like clockwork, I clean my house. Watering plants, dusting, sweeping, mopping and vacuuming are just a few of my rituals. After all my chores are done I retreat to my living room. Circling chairs, praying, worshiping and preparing has become such a special time in my day.

Around 6:00 p.m. every Tuesday night the ladies begin arriving. Women from different denominations, walks of life, stages of life and situations in life gather. We gather together to worship. We worship in song. We learn from His Word. We apply the scripture to our everyday situations and circumstances. We pray. We assemble in great expectation of what God will do in and through us.

Several years ago, God challenged me to open my home and invite women from the community to meet as a sisterhood. I did just that. Called to help people, He continually brought hurting, broken, confused, desperate, challenged, believing and non-believing women into my life. Wanting to make a difference, I gladly accepted the challenge. Every woman that came expected Him to meet her needs. We were challenged to believe His Word and we were moved to a deeper faith.

Over the years I have seen Him do exactly what His Word says He will do. I've witnessed firsthand, His hand; heal the sick, open the eyes of the blind in spirit, restore marriages, deliver addictions, set captives free, bind up the brokenhearted, receive Jesus as Savior, experience a break though and so much more. He has never failed us! In His mightiness we have recovered. We have been ministered to in the very depths of our hearts, minds, and souls. There is no one greater than our God!

God's intentions are to meet our needs. In fact, He wants to meet EVERY ONE of them. Our dependence on Him is such to our benefit. In times of desperation or the need to know and trust Him on a deeper level, He is ready and waiting. He wants to be everything to His children for whom He calls woman!

What is it today that you need from your Heavenly Father? Is there a church or ladies group nearby where perhaps He can minister to you? Has He called you to open up your home as a safe haven for the lost, hurting and broken? Take time today to ask God to show you where you fit. Allow Him to lead you, guide you, position you and purpose you for greatness!

*"Therefore go and make disciples of all nations, baptizing them in the name of the Father and of the Son and of the Holy Spirit, and teaching them to obey everything I have commanded you. And surely I am with you always to the very end of the age."*
*Matthew 28:19-20 (NIV)*

# THE PROGRESSION OF HER LIFE

*S*he was at the end of her rope. Her addiction, her grief, and her struggles were drowning her. Her final arrest that September morning literally saved her life!

This 27-year-old woman had suffered an extremely difficult life. Her mother and father had lived out drug addiction since her birth. After several years of unresolved issues her mom and dad finally divorced and this young girl was forced to be swapped back and forth from house to house and parent to parent. That eventually takes a toll on a young girl. A big toll!

In the midst of dysfunction, the pain tends to cause a person to make choices that cover up and drown the hurt. Her pain was no exception. Her first taste of alcohol as a teenager immediately masked her feelings. She was instantly hooked and honestly, more than she even knew!

Alcohol leads to drugs, and for women, drugs can then lead to men. Men lead to children. That was the exact progression of her life. At 24 years of age, she was raising children and pregnant again when another tragedy struck. On that Father's day, her daddy was tragically killed in a car crash. Being a daddy's girl made his death even more of a heartache. In then just four short months later, another horrific event took place in her life. Her husband was found dead after an unpredicted overdose. At this point, her whole world came crashing down. Overwhelmed and overcome with grief and disbelief, prescription pain pills become her norm. Addiction and prostitution made their bed in her everyday life. All hope was gone along with the two men that meant the most to her. In reality, nothing mattered to her anymore!

When I met her, she was checking into the treatment center where I was the director. Not only had she lost her daddy and her husband, but time, pills and prostitution had stolen her children too. . . . all three of them. She had never known there was a God that could save her but she was about to find out.

The following Sunday, we attended a local church service and this woman surrendered her heart to God. He was her only hope. He was the only one that could mend her broken heart and put the pieces back into place. Although after a few months she left treatment and went back to some places from where God had delivered her.

One year later, I received a call from her as she was being booked into the county jail. Remembering my number, she reached out. She knew it was time to finally allow God total control of every aspect of her life. Returning to treatment, made all the difference. She graduated from the program and we watched God restore almost everything she had lost.

Today, two years later, this precious woman is a new creation in Christ! She has met the man of her dreams and is scheduled to marry within the coming year. The court has granted visitation for her children and she is in the process of getting back full custody. All of the things in life that cause your heart to beat again have been restored to her. Most of all, she restored her relationship with her Savior! Her great God has helped her to let go of all of the pain and hurt in her life and replace it with the joy of her salvation. He has set her free from the chains of addiction and He is bringing to completion what He began in her despite her circumstances.

God wants to restore your life as well. Crippled by the pain of your past, overcome from the destruction of your circumstances, God is still in the miracle business. He wants to bring about the resurrection of your deadness by breathing new life into it.

What is it today that God can redo or renew for you? Are their situations, circumstances or tragic events that need to be restored? Take time today to allow Him to hold you. Allow Him to be the Father He wants to be. In His time, through His mercy and grace, He will make all of your destruction new. He will bring restoration like you've never known before. He will bring beauty from your ashes! Let Him have your pile and see what He can do.

> *"to bestow on them a crown of beauty instead of ashes, the oil of joy instead of mourning, and a garment of praise instead of a spirit of despair. They will be called oaks of righteousness, a planting of the Lord for the display of his splendor. They will rebuild the ancient ruins and restore the places long devastated; they will renew the ruined cities that have been devastated for generations.*
> *Isaiah 61:3&4 (NIV)*

# WHERE WILL I GO FROM HERE?

*A*s I conclude this devotional, I can't help but ponder what happens from here. Reflecting on my days gone by, some I can't seem to remember and yet others I will never forget. Every circumstance, every person, every situation and every good and bad event has played an incredible role in positioning me for what lies ahead.

I have spent the majority of my years trying to live as I am convicted by how God has called me to live. Sadly, most of the time I have failed. Fortunately, because of Christ, my mistakes, disobedience and rebellious ways have been forgiven. My learning, my living and my seasoning are the reason I trust my Savior.

There isn't anything I can do to change my history. There are choices I have made that I still wish now I had not chosen. There are ways in which I acted and things I said I wish I could retract. These things remain in my past but it is not a reflection of who I am today. It is a stepping-stone to learning and challenging who I have become. Without the harsh reality of my actions and less than loveable behavior, my challenges to be more like Christ would be futile.

Daily, I choose to allow God to perfect me. The more I seek Him, the more like Him I become. Even though sometimes I would like to operate in the flesh (stomp my feet and fuss), I'm quickly jerked back into the reality of the consequences of my actions. I have learned to "play the tape until the end"! To be like Christ requires sacrifice; sacrifice of the flesh. Do I always get it right? NO! Every day I have to examine my ways, test my thoughts and ask God to purify me all over again.

The odds are that if you're reading this, I know you. And then again, maybe I don't. Regardless, I hope you see that through every thread of my story, God has been there. He is into details! In fact, He has worked every detail out in my obedient and disobedient days. He wants to do the same in yours!

My prayer today is that you know him also. Even if you have chosen to walk away from Him, blame Him, deny Him, turn your back on Him or refuse to accept Him, He still desires to get 'in your business.' No matter how many steps you've taken while walking away, it only takes one step back to Him! God wants to take over and show you the rest of your story as He sees it! He wants to satisfy your heart while you become complete and whole in Him. He desires that you allow HIM to be your Father!

I have included the following prayer for you to recite if you recognize that your life has been better or will be better in His Hands. I pray that from the moment you receive Christ or perhaps rededicate your life to Him, you will never be the same. I pray you will see that having a new heart in Him will finally satisfy that empty spot inside of you that you've spent your entire life trying to fill. He is the ONLY one that can truly fill it!

*Father God, I know that I am a sinner. I know that I am in need of a Savior. I believe you were crucified on the cross, buried and rose again on the third day. I ask you to come into my heart and cleanse me of all the sin in my life. I thank you God for changing me and making me whole. Today, I commit to serving you and telling others about you. Thank you Lord for saving my soul!*

Congratulations!

If you said this prayer, I will meet you in Heaven if not before then! Please tell someone close to you about your decision and get involved in a local church. Your spiritual growth requires spiritual food and the support of other believers. I rejoice with you in your decision!!!

*"For God so loved the world that He gave His one and only Son,*
*that whoever believes in Him shall not perish but have eternal life.*
*For God did not send His Son into the world to condemn the world,*
*but to save the world through Him.*
*John 3:16 & 17 (NIV)*

CPSIA information can be obtained
at www.ICGtesting.com
Printed in the USA
LVHW061321180723
752727LV00014B/1265